HOUGHTON MIFFLIN HARCOURT

MATH Expressions
Common Core

Dr. Karen C. Fuson

GRADE  3

 This material is based upon work supported by the
National Science Foundation
under Grant Numbers
ESI-9816320, REC-9806020, and RED-935373.

Any opinions, findings, and conclusions, or recommendations expressed in this material
are those of the author and do not necessarily reflect the views of the National Science Foundation.

 HOUGHTON MIFFLIN HARCOURT

Printed in the U.S.A.

ISBN: 978-0-547-82415-4

7 8 9 10   0868   21 20 19 18 17 16 15 14 13

4500413363   A B C D E F G

CONTENTS

UNIT 1 Multiplication and Division with 0–5, 9 and 10

1 Multiply with 5................... 1

FAMILY LETTER............ 1

3 Multiplication and Arrays.......... 5

FAMILY LETTER............ 5

5 Multiply and Divide with 2........ 13

6 Building Fluency with 2s and 5s.... 15

8 Multiply and Divide with 9........ 17

9 Building Fluency with 2s, 5s, 9s, and 10s..................... 19

11 Multiplication and Area........... 21

12 Multiply and Divide with 4........ 49

13 Use the Strategy Cards........... 51

17 Play Multiplication and Division Games................. 53

18 Building Fluency with 0s, 1s, 2s, 3s, 4s, 5s, 9s, 10s............. 59

19 Focus on Mathematical Practices... 65

UNIT 1 Test.............. 67

UNIT 2 Multiplication and Division with 6s, 7s, 8s and Multiply with Multiples of 10

1 Multiply and Divide with 6....... 69

FAMILY LETTER........... 69

2 Solve Area Word Problems........ 71

3 Multiply and Divide with 8....... 73

4 Write Word Problems and Equations.................. 75

6 Square Numbers.............. 77

7 Practice with 6s, 7s, and 8s....... 79

8 Building Fluency with 0s–10s...... 83

13 Play Multiplication and Division Games................. 91

14 Building Fluency with 0s–10s..... 111

UNIT 2 Test............. 113

UNIT 3 Measurement, Time, and Graphs

1 Customary Units of Length....... 115

FAMILY LETTER........... 115

2 Customary Units of Liquid Volume................. 119

3 Metric Units of Liquid Volume.... 121

4 Customary Units of Weight and Metric Units of Mass........ 123

6 Tell Time.................. 127

FAMILY LETTER........... 127

9 Add and Subtract Time.......... 133

11 Read and Create Pictographs and Bar Graphs................ 135

FAMILY LETTER........... 135

12 Read and Create Bar Graphs with Multidigit Numbers......... 139

13 Represent and Organize Data..... 141

15 Focus on Mathematical Practices.. 143

UNIT 3 Test............. 145

© Houghton Mifflin Harcourt Publishing Company

CONTENTS (continued)

UNIT 4 Multidigit Addition and Subtraction

1. Make Place Value Drawings 119
   - FAMILY LETTER 119
2. Build Numbers 153
   - ✓ UNIT 4 Test 157

UNIT 5 Write Equations to Solve Word Problems

1. Addition and Subtraction Situations 159
   - FAMILY LETTER 159
   - ✓ UNIT 5 Test 161

UNIT 6 Polygons, Perimeter, and Area

1. Triangles 163
   - FAMILY LETTER 163
3. Draw Quadrilaterals.......... 167
4. Classify Quadrilaterals 171

5. Perimeter and Area 177
   - FAMILY LETTER 177
6. Side Lengths with Area and Perimeter.................. 185
7. Compare Areas and Perimeters.... 187
8. Area of Rectilinear Figures 189
10. Tangram Shapes and Area........ 193
11. Focus on Mathematical Practices .. 201
    - ✓ UNIT 6 Test 203

UNIT 7 Explore Fractions

1. Understand Fractions........... 207
   - FAMILY LETTER 207
2. Model Fractions 213
3. Locate Fractions on the Number Line................. 215
5. Compare Fractions 219
6. Introduce Equivalence 221
7. Equivalent Fractions........... 223
   - ✓ UNIT 7 Test 225

Family Letter

Dear Family,

In this unit and the next, your child will be practicing basic multiplications and divisions. *Math Expressions* incorporates studying, practicing, and testing of the basic multiplications and divisions in class. Your child is also expected to practice at home.

Homework Helper Your child will have math homework almost every day. He or she needs a Homework Helper. The helper may be anyone — you, an older brother or sister (or other family member), a neighbor, or a friend. Please decide who the main Homework Helper will be and ask your child to tell the teacher tomorrow. Make a specific time for homework and provide your child with a quiet place to work.

Study Plans Each day your child will fill out a study plan, indicating which basic multiplications and divisions he or she will study that evening. When your child has finished studying (practicing), his or her Homework Helper should sign the study plan.

1–1 **Homework**	Name		Date
Study Plan			
			Homework Helper

Practice Charts Each time a new number is introduced, students' homework will include a practice chart. To practice, students can cover the products with a pencil or a strip of heavy paper. They will say the multiplications, sliding the pencil or paper down the column to see each product after saying it. Students can also start with the last problem in a column and slide up. It is important that your child studies count-bys and multiplications at least 5 minutes every night. Your child can also use these charts to practice division on the mixed up column by covering the first factor.

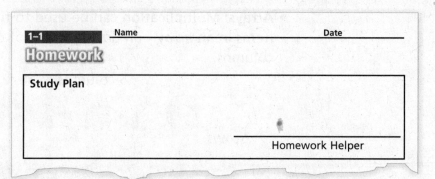

	In Order	Mixed Up
5s	1 × 5 = 5	9 × 5 = 45
	2 × 5 = 10	5 × 5 = 25
	3 × 5 = 15	2 × 5 = 10
	4 × 5 = 20	7 × 5 = 35
	5 × 5 = 25	4 × 5 = 20
	6 × 5 = 30	6 × 5 = 30
	7 × 5 = 35	10 × 5 = 50
	8 × 5 = 40	8 × 5 = 40
	9 × 5 = 45	1 × 5 = 5
	10 × 5 = 50	3 × 5 = 15

To help students understand the concept of multiplication, the *Math Expressions* program presents three ways to think about multiplication.

- **Repeated groups**: Multiplication can be used to find the total in repeated groups of the same size. In early lessons, students circle the group size in repeated-groups equations to help keep track of which factor is the group size and which is the number of groups.

4 groups of bananas

$4 \times ③ = 3 + 3 + 3 + 3 = 12$

- **Arrays**: Multiplication can be used to find the total number of items in an *array*—an arrangement of objects into rows and columns.

5 columns

2 rows 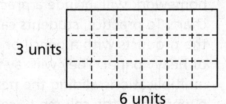 2-by-5 array

2 rows of pennies = $2 \times 5 = 10$

- **Area**: Multiplication can be used to find the area of a rectangle.

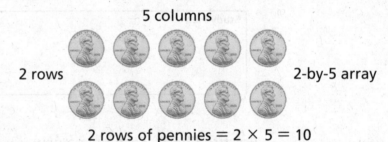

3 units

6 units

Area: 3 units × 6 units = 18 square units

Please call if you have any questions or comments.

Thank you.

Sincerely,
Your child's teacher

COMMON CORE This unit includes the Common Core Standards for Mathematical Content for Operations and Algebraic Thinking, 3.OA.1, 3.OA.2, 3.OA.3, 3.OA.4, 3.OA.5, 3.OA.6, 3.OA.7, 3.OA.9, Measurement and Data, 3.MD.5a, 3.MD.5b, 3.MD.7a, 3.MD.7b, 3.MD.7c, 3.MD.7d, and all Mathematical Practices.

Estimada familia:

En esta unidad y en la que sigue, su niño practicará multiplicaciones y divisiones básicas. *Math Expressions* incorpora en la clase el estudio, la práctica y la evaluación de las multiplicaciones y divisiones básicas. También se espera que su niño practique en casa.

Ayudante de tareas Su niño tendrá tarea de matemáticas casi a diario y necesitará un ayudante para hacer sus tareas. Ese ayudante puede ser cualquier persona: usted, un hermano o hermana mayor, otro familiar, un vecino o un amigo. Por favor decida quién será esta persona y pida a su niño que se lo diga a su maestro mañana. Designe un tiempo específico para la tarea y un lugar para trabajar sin distracciones.

Planes de estudio Todos los días su niño va a completar un plan de estudio, que indica cuáles multiplicaciones y divisiones debe estudiar esa noche. Cuando su niño haya terminado de estudiar (practicar), la persona que lo ayude debe firmar el plan de estudio.

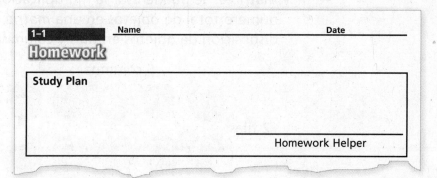

Tablas de práctica Cada vez que se presente un número nuevo, la tarea de los estudiantes incluirá una tabla de práctica. Para practicar, los estudiantes pueden cubrir los productos con un lápiz o una tira de papel grueso. Los niños dicen la multiplicación y deslizan el lápiz o el papel hacia abajo para revelar el producto después de decirlo. También pueden empezar con el último problema de la columna y deslizar el lápiz o el papel hacia arriba. Es importante que su niño practique el conteo y la multiplicación por lo menos 5 minutos cada noche. Su niño también puede usar estas tablas para practicar la división en la columna de productos desordenados cubriendo el primer factor.

	En orden	Desordenados
5	1 × 5 = 5	9 × 5 = 45
	2 × 5 = 10	5 × 5 = 25
	3 × 5 = 15	2 × 5 = 10
	4 × 5 = 20	7 × 5 = 35
	5 × 5 = 25	4 × 5 = 20
	6 × 5 = 30	6 × 5 = 30
	7 × 5 = 35	10 × 5 = 50
	8 × 5 = 40	8 × 5 = 40
	9 × 5 = 45	1 × 5 = 5
	10 × 5 = 50	3 × 5 = 15

Para ayudar a los estudiantes a comprender el concepto de la multiplicación, el programa *Math Expressions* presenta tres maneras de pensar en la multiplicación. Éstas se describen a continuación.

- **Grupos repetidos**: La multiplicación se puede usar para hallar el total con grupos del mismo tamaño que se repiten. Cuando empiezan a trabajar con ecuaciones de grupos repetidos, los estudiantes rodean con un círculo el tamaño del grupo en las ecuaciones, para recordar cuál factor representa el tamaño del grupo y cuál representa el número de grupos.

4 grupos de bananas

$4 \times ③ = 3 + 3 + 3 + 3 = 12$

- **Matrices**: Se puede usar la multiplicación para hallar el número total de objetos en una *matriz*, es decir, una disposición de objetos en filas y columnas.

5 columnas

2 filas   matriz de 2 por 5

2 filas de monedas de un centavo $= 2 \times 5 = 10$

- **Área**: Se puede usar la multiplicación para hallar el área de un rectángulo.

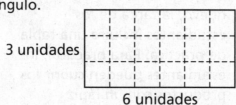

3 unidades

6 unidades

Área: 3 unidades $\times$ 6 unidades $= 18$ unidades cuadradas

Si tiene alguna duda o algún comentario, por favor comuníquese conmigo. Gracias.

Atentamente,
El maestro de su niño

COMMON CORE La Unidad 1 incluye los Common Core Standards for Mathematical Content for Operations and Algebraic Thinking, 3.OA.1, 3.OA.2, 3.OA.3, 3.OA.4, 3.OA.5, 3.OA.6, 3.OA.7, 3.OA.9, Measurement and Data, 3.MD.5a, 3.MD.5b, 3.MD.7a, 3.MD.7b, 3.MD.7c, 3.MD.7d, and all Mathematical Practices.

Family Letter

Dear Family,

In addition to practice charts for the basic multiplications and divisions for each of the numbers 1 through 10, your child will bring home a variety of other practice materials over the next several weeks.

• **Home Study Sheets:** A Home Study Sheet includes 3 or 4 practice charts on one page. Your child can use the Home Study Sheets to practice all the count-bys, multiplications, and divisions for a number or to practice just the ones he or she doesn't know for that number. The Homework Helper can then use the sheet to test (or retest) your child. The Homework Helper should check with your child to see which basic multiplications or divisions he or she is ready to be tested on. The helper should mark any missed problems lightly with a pencil.

If your child gets all the answers in a column correct, the helper should sign that column on the Home Signature Sheet. When signatures are on all the columns of the Home Signature Sheet, your child should bring the sheet to school.

Home Study Sheet A

5s			2s		
Count-bys	Mixed Up ×	Mixed Up ÷	Count-bys	Mixed Up ×	Mixed Up ÷
1 × 5 = 5	2 × 5 = 10	10 ÷ 5 = 2	1 × 2 = 2	7 × 2 = 14	20 ÷ 2 = 10
2 × 5 = 10	9 × 5 = 45	35 ÷ 5 = 7	2 × 2 = 4	1 × 2 = 2	2 ÷ 2 = 1
3 × 5 = 15	1 × 5 = 5	50 ÷ 5 = 10	3 × 2 = 6	3 × 2 = 6	6 ÷ 2 = 3
4 × 5 = 20	5 × 5 = 25	5 ÷ 5 = 1	4 × 2 = 8	5 × 2 = 10	16 ÷ 2 = 8
5 × 5 = 25	7 × 5 = 35	20 ÷ 5 = 4	5 × 2 = 10	6 × 2 = 12	12 ÷ 2 = 6
6 × 5 = 30	3 × 5 = 15	15 ÷ 5 = 3	6 × 2 = 12	8 × 2 = 16	4 ÷ 2 = 2
7 × 5 = 35	10 × 5 = 50	30 ÷ 5 = 6	7 × 2 = 14	2 × 2 = 4	10 ÷ 2 = 5
8 × 5 = 40	6 × 5 = 30	40 ÷ 5 = 8	8 × 2 = 16	10 × 2 = 20	8 ÷ 2 = 4
9 × 5 = 45	4 × 5 = 20	25 ÷ 5 = 5	9 × 2 = 18	4 × 2 = 8	14 ÷ 2 = 7
10 × 5 = 50	8 × 5 = 40	45 ÷ 5 = 9	10 × 2 = 20	9 × 2 = 18	18 ÷ 2 = 9

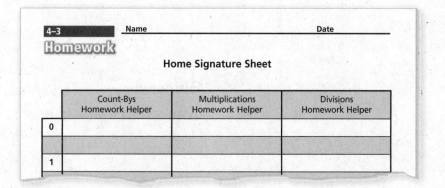

4–3

Homework

Name _____ Date _____

Home Signature Sheet

	Count-Bys Homework Helper	Multiplications Homework Helper	Divisions Homework Helper
0			
1			

Multiplication and Arrays **5**

- **Home Check Sheets:** A Home Check Sheet includes columns of 20 multiplications and divisions in mixed order. These sheets can be used to test your student's fluency with basic facts.

- **Strategy Cards:** Students use Strategy Cards in class as flashcards, to play games, and to develop multiplication and division strategies.

Sample Multiplication Card   **Sample Division Card**

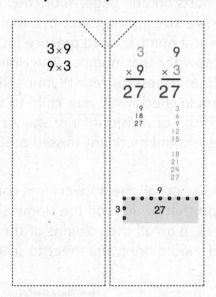   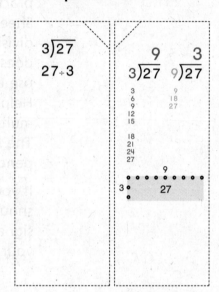

- **Games:** Near the end of this unit, students are introduced to games that provide multiplication and division practice.

Encourage your child to show you these materials and explain how they are used. Make sure your child spends time practicing multiplications and divisions every evening.

Please call if you have any questions or comments.

Thank you.

Sincerely,
Your child's teacher

This unit includes the Common Core Standards for Mathematical Content for Operations and Algebraic Thinking, 3.OA.1, 3.OA.2, 3.OA.3, 3.OA.4, 3.OA.5, 3.OA.6, 3.OA.7, 3.OA.9, Measurement and Data, 3.MD.5a, 3.MD.5b, 3.MD.7a, 3.MD.7b, 3.MD.7c, 3.MD.7d, and all Mathematical Practices.

Estimada familia:

Además de las tablas de práctica para las multiplicaciones y divisiones básicas para cada número del 1 al 10, su niño llevará a casa una variedad de materiales de práctica en las semanas que vienen.

• **Hojas para estudiar en casa:** Una hoja para estudiar en casa incluye 3 ó 4 tablas de práctica en una página. Su niño puede usar las hojas para practicar todos los conteos, multiplicaciones y divisiones de un número, o para practicar sólo las operaciones para ese número que no domine. La persona que ayude a su niño con la tarea puede usar la hoja para hacerle una prueba (o repetir una prueba). Esa persona debe hablar con su niño para decidir sobre qué multiplicaciones o divisiones básicas el niño puede hacer la prueba. La persona que ayude debe marcar ligeramente con un lápiz cualquier problema que conteste mal. Si su niño contesta bien todas las operaciones de una columna, la persona que ayude debe firmar esa columna de la hoja de firmas. Cuando todas las columnas de la hoja de firmas estén firmadas, su niño debe llevar la hoja a la escuela.

Home Study Sheet A

5s			2s		
Count-bys	Mixed Up ×	Mixed Up ÷	Count-bys	Mixed Up ×	Mixed Up ÷
1 × 5 = 5	2 × 5 = 10	10 ÷ 5 = 2	1 × 2 = 2	7 × 2 = 14	20 ÷ 2 = 10
2 × 5 = 10	9 × 5 = 45	35 ÷ 5 = 7	2 × 2 = 4	1 × 2 = 2	2 ÷ 2 = 1
3 × 5 = 15	1 × 5 = 5	50 ÷ 5 = 10	3 × 2 = 6	3 × 2 = 6	6 ÷ 2 = 3
4 × 5 = 20	5 × 5 = 25	5 ÷ 5 = 1	4 × 2 = 8	5 × 2 = 10	16 ÷ 2 = 8
5 × 5 = 25	7 × 5 = 35	20 ÷ 5 = 4	5 × 2 = 10	6 × 2 = 12	12 ÷ 2 = 6
6 × 5 = 30	3 × 5 = 15	15 ÷ 5 = 3	6 × 2 = 12	8 × 2 = 16	4 ÷ 2 = 2
7 × 5 = 35	10 × 5 = 50	30 ÷ 5 = 6	7 × 2 = 14	2 × 2 = 4	10 ÷ 2 = 5
8 × 5 = 40	6 × 5 = 30	40 ÷ 5 = 8	8 × 2 = 16	10 × 2 = 20	8 ÷ 2 = 4
9 × 5 = 45	4 × 5 = 20	25 ÷ 5 = 5	9 × 2 = 18	4 × 2 = 8	14 ÷ 2 = 7
10 × 5 = 50	8 × 5 = 40	45 ÷ 5 = 9	10 × 2 = 20	9 × 2 = 18	18 ÷ 2 = 9

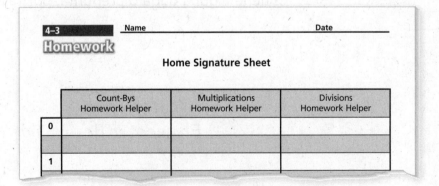

4-3

Homework

Name _____   Date _____

Home Signature Sheet

	Count-Bys Homework Helper	Multiplications Homework Helper	Divisions Homework Helper
0			
1			

Multiplication and Arrays **7**

Carta a la familia

- **Hojas de verificación:** Una hoja de verificación consta de columnas de 20 multiplicaciones y divisiones sin orden fijo. Estas hojas pueden usarse para comprobar el dominio de las operaciones básicas.

- **Tarjetas de estrategias:** Los estudiantes usan las tarjetas de estrategias en la clase como ayuda de memoria, en juegos y para desarrollar estrategias para hacer multiplicaciones y divisiones.

Ejemplo de tarjeta de multiplicación   **Ejemplo de tarjeta de división**

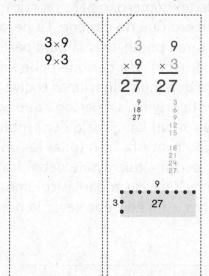   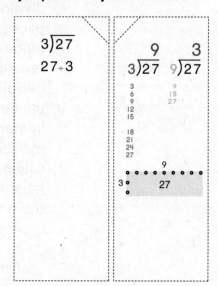

- **Juegos:** Hacia el final de esta unidad se presentan juegos a los estudiantes para practicar la multiplicación y la división.

Anime a su niño a que le muestre estos materiales y a que le explique cómo se usan. Asegúrese de que su niño practique la multiplicación y la división cada noche.

Si tiene alguna duda o pregunta, por favor comuníquese conmigo.

Atentamente,
El maestro de su niño

COMMON CORE   La Unidad 1 incluye los Common Core Standards for Mathematical Content for Operations and Algebraic Thinking, 3.OA.1, 3.OA.2, 3.OA.3, 3.OA.4, 3.OA.5, 3.OA.6, 3.OA.7, 3.OA.9, Measurement and Data, 3.MD.5a, 3.MD.5b, 3.MD.7a, 3.MD.7b, 3.MD.7c, 3.MD.7d, and all Mathematical Practices.

Signature Sheet

	Count-Bys Partner	Multiplications Partner	Divisions Partner	Multiplications Check Sheets	Divisions Check Sheets
5s				1:	1:
2s				1:	1:
10s				2:	2:
9s				2:	2:
				3:	3:
3s				4:	4:
4s				4:	4:
1s				5:	5:
0s				5:	5:
				6:	6:
6s				7:	7:
8s				7:	7:
7s				8:	8:
				9:	9:
				10:	10:

1-3
Class Activity

Name

Date

Dash Record Sheet

Dash Number	Accurate	Fast	Really Fast		Dash Number	Accurate	Fast	Really Fast
1					13			
2					14			
3					15			
4					16			
5					17			
6					18			
7					19			
8					19A			
9					19B			
9A					19C			
9B					19D			
9C					20			
10					20A			
10A					20B			
10B					20C			
10C					20D			
11					21			
11A					21A			
11B					21B			
11C					21C			
12					22			
12A					22A			
12B					22B			
12C					22C			

© Houghton Mifflin Harcourt Publishing Company

10 UNIT 1 LESSON 3

Dash Record Sheet

Name _____ Date _____

Study Sheet A

5s

Count-bys	Mixed Up ×	Mixed Up ÷
1 × 5 = 5	2 × 5 = 10	10 ÷ 5 = 2
2 × 5 = 10	9 × 5 = 45	35 ÷ 5 = 7
3 × 5 = 15	1 × 5 = 5	50 ÷ 5 = 10
4 × 5 = 20	5 × 5 = 25	5 ÷ 5 = 1
5 × 5 = 25	7 × 5 = 35	20 ÷ 5 = 4
6 × 5 = 30	3 × 5 = 15	15 ÷ 5 = 3
7 × 5 = 35	10 × 5 = 50	30 ÷ 5 = 6
8 × 5 = 40	6 × 5 = 30	40 ÷ 5 = 8
9 × 5 = 45	4 × 5 = 20	25 ÷ 5 = 5
10 × 5 = 50	8 × 5 = 40	45 ÷ 5 = 9

2s

Count-bys	Mixed Up ×	Mixed Up ÷
1 × 2 = 2	7 × 2 = 14	20 ÷ 2 = 10
2 × 2 = 4	1 × 2 = 2	2 ÷ 2 = 1
3 × 2 = 6	3 × 2 = 6	6 ÷ 2 = 3
4 × 2 = 8	5 × 2 = 10	16 ÷ 2 = 8
5 × 2 = 10	6 × 2 = 12	12 ÷ 2 = 6
6 × 2 = 12	8 × 2 = 16	4 ÷ 2 = 2
7 × 2 = 14	2 × 2 = 4	10 ÷ 2 = 5
8 × 2 = 16	10 × 2 = 20	8 ÷ 2 = 4
9 × 2 = 18	4 × 2 = 8	14 ÷ 2 = 7
10 × 2 = 20	9 × 2 = 18	18 ÷ 2 = 9

10s

Count-bys	Mixed Up ×	Mixed Up ÷
1 × 10 = 10	1 × 10 = 10	80 ÷ 10 = 8
2 × 10 = 20	5 × 10 = 50	10 ÷ 10 = 1
3 × 10 = 30	2 × 10 = 20	50 ÷ 10 = 5
4 × 10 = 40	8 × 10 = 80	90 ÷ 10 = 9
5 × 10 = 50	7 × 10 = 70	40 ÷ 10 = 4
6 × 10 = 60	3 × 10 = 30	100 ÷ 10 = 10
7 × 10 = 70	4 × 10 = 40	30 ÷ 10 = 3
8 × 10 = 80	6 × 10 = 60	20 ÷ 10 = 2
9 × 10 = 90	10 × 10 = 100	70 ÷ 10 = 7
10 × 10 = 100	9 × 10 = 90	60 ÷ 10 = 6

9s

Count-bys	Mixed Up ×	Mixed Up ÷
1 × 9 = 9	2 × 9 = 18	81 ÷ 9 = 9
2 × 9 = 18	4 × 9 = 36	18 ÷ 9 = 2
3 × 9 = 27	7 × 9 = 63	36 ÷ 9 = 4
4 × 9 = 36	8 × 9 = 72	9 ÷ 9 = 1
5 × 9 = 45	3 × 9 = 27	54 ÷ 9 = 6
6 × 9 = 54	10 × 9 = 90	27 ÷ 9 = 3
7 × 9 = 63	1 × 9 = 9	63 ÷ 9 = 7
8 × 9 = 72	6 × 9 = 54	72 ÷ 9 = 8
9 × 9 = 81	5 × 9 = 45	90 ÷ 9 = 10
10 × 9 = 90	9 × 9 = 81	45 ÷ 9 = 5

► **PATH to FLUENCY** **Check Sheet 1: 5s and 2s**

5s Multiplications	5s Divisions	2s Multiplications	2s Divisions
$2 \times 5 = 10$	$30 / 5 = 6$	$4 \times 2 = 8$	$8 / 2 = 4$
$5 \cdot 6 = 30$	$5 \div 5 = 1$	$2 \cdot 8 = 16$	$18 \div 2 = 9$
$5 * 9 = 45$	$15 / 5 = 3$	$1 * 2 = 2$	$2 / 2 = 1$
$4 \times 5 = 20$	$50 \div 5 = 10$	$6 \times 2 = 12$	$16 \div 2 = 8$
$5 \cdot 7 = 35$	$20 / 5 = 4$	$2 \cdot 9 = 18$	$4 / 2 = 2$
$10 * 5 = 50$	$10 \div 5 = 2$	$2 * 2 = 4$	$20 \div 2 = 10$
$1 \times 5 = 5$	$35 / 5 = 7$	$3 \times 2 = 6$	$10 / 2 = 5$
$5 \cdot 3 = 15$	$40 \div 5 = 8$	$2 \cdot 5 = 10$	$12 \div 2 = 6$
$8 * 5 = 40$	$25 / 5 = 5$	$10 * 2 = 20$	$6 / 2 = 3$
$5 \times 5 = 25$	$45 / 5 = 9$	$2 \times 7 = 14$	$14 / 2 = 7$
$5 \cdot 8 = 40$	$20 \div 5 = 4$	$2 \cdot 10 = 20$	$4 \div 2 = 2$
$7 * 5 = 35$	$15 / 5 = 3$	$9 * 2 = 18$	$2 / 2 = 1$
$5 \times 4 = 20$	$30 \div 5 = 6$	$2 \times 6 = 12$	$8 \div 2 = 4$
$6 \cdot 5 = 30$	$25 / 5 = 5$	$8 \cdot 2 = 16$	$6 / 2 = 3$
$5 * 1 = 5$	$10 \div 5 = 2$	$2 * 3 = 6$	$20 \div 2 = 10$
$5 \times 10 = 50$	$45 / 5 = 9$	$2 \times 2 = 4$	$14 / 2 = 7$
$9 \cdot 5 = 45$	$35 \div 5 = 7$	$1 \cdot 2 = 2$	$10 \div 2 = 5$
$5 * 2 = 10$	$50 \div 5 = 10$	$2 * 4 = 8$	$16 \div 2 = 8$
$3 \times 5 = 15$	$40 / 5 = 8$	$5 \times 2 = 10$	$12 / 2 = 6$
$5 \cdot 5 = 25$	$5 \div 5 = 1$	$7 \cdot 2 = 14$	$18 \div 2 = 9$

▶ **PATH to FLUENCY** **Use the Target**

×	0	1	2	3	4	5	6	7	8	9
0	0	0	0	0	0	0	0	0	0	0
1	0	1	2	3	4	5	6	7	8	9
2	0	2	4	6	8	10	12	14	16	18
3	0	3	6	9	12	15	18	21	24	27
4	0	4	8	12	16	20	24	28	32	36
5	0	5	10	15	20	25	30	35	40	45
6	0	6	12	18	24	30	36	42	48	54
7	0	7	14	21	28	35	42	49	56	63
8	0	8	16	24	32	40	48	56	64	72
9	0	9	18	27	36	45	54	63	72	81

1. Discuss how you can use the Target to find the product for 8×5.

2. Discuss how you can use the Target to practice division.

3. Practice using the Target.

4. When using the Target, how are multiplication and division alike? How are they different?

_____

_____

_____

_____

Name _____   Date _____

► **PATH to FLUENCY** **Check Sheet 2: 10s and 9s**

10s Multiplications	10s Divisions	9s Multiplications	9s Divisions
$9 \times 10 = 90$	$100 / 10 = 10$	$3 \times 9 = 27$	$27 / 9 = 3$
$10 \cdot 3 = 30$	$50 \div 10 = 5$	$9 \cdot 7 = 63$	$9 \div 9 = 1$
$10 * 6 = 60$	$70 / 10 = 7$	$10 * 9 = 90$	$81 / 9 = 9$
$1 \times 10 = 10$	$40 \div 10 = 4$	$5 \times 9 = 45$	$45 \div 9 = 5$
$10 \cdot 4 = 40$	$80 / 10 = 8$	$9 \cdot 8 = 72$	$90 / 9 = 10$
$10 * 7 = 70$	$60 \div 10 = 6$	$9 * 1 = 9$	$36 \div 9 = 4$
$8 \times 10 = 80$	$10 / 10 = 1$	$2 \times 9 = 18$	$18 / 9 = 2$
$10 \cdot 10 = 100$	$20 \div 10 = 2$	$9 \cdot 9 = 81$	$63 \div 9 = 7$
$5 * 10 = 50$	$90 / 10 = 9$	$6 * 9 = 54$	$54 / 9 = 6$
$10 \times 2 = 20$	$30 / 10 = 3$	$9 \times 4 = 36$	$72 / 9 = 8$
$10 \cdot 5 = 50$	$80 \div 10 = 8$	$9 \cdot 5 = 45$	$27 \div 9 = 3$
$4 * 10 = 40$	$70 / 10 = 7$	$4 * 9 = 36$	$45 / 9 = 5$
$10 \times 1 = 10$	$100 \div 10 = 10$	$9 \times 1 = 9$	$63 \div 9 = 7$
$3 \cdot 10 = 30$	$90 / 10 = 9$	$3 \cdot 9 = 27$	$72 / 9 = 8$
$10 * 8 = 80$	$60 \div 10 = 6$	$9 * 8 = 72$	$54 \div 9 = 6$
$7 \times 10 = 70$	$30 / 10 = 3$	$7 \times 9 = 63$	$18 / 9 = 2$
$6 \cdot 10 = 60$	$10 \div 10 = 1$	$6 \cdot 9 = 54$	$90 \div 9 = 10$
$10 * 9 = 90$	$40 \div 10 = 4$	$9 * 9 = 81$	$9 \div 9 = 1$
$10 \times 10 = 100$	$20 / 10 = 2$	$10 \times 9 = 90$	$36 / 9 = 4$
$2 \cdot 10 = 20$	$50 \div 10 = 5$	$2 \cdot 9 = 18$	$81 \div 9 = 9$

▶ **PATH to FLUENCY** **Check Sheet 3: 2s, 5s, 9s, and 10s**

2s, 5s, 9s, 10s Multiplications	2s, 5s, 9s, 10s Multiplications	2s, 5s, 9s, 10s Divisions	2s, 5s, 9s, 10s Divisions
$2 \times 10 = 20$	$5 \times 10 = 50$	$18 / 2 = 9$	$36 / 9 = 4$
$10 \cdot 5 = 50$	$10 \cdot 9 = 90$	$50 \div 5 = 10$	$70 \div 10 = 7$
$9 * 6 = 54$	$4 * 10 = 40$	$72 / 9 = 8$	$18 / 2 = 9$
$7 \times 10 = 70$	$2 \times 9 = 18$	$60 \div 10 = 6$	$45 \div 5 = 9$
$2 \cdot 3 = 6$	$5 \cdot 3 = 15$	$12 / 2 = 6$	$45 / 9 = 5$
$5 * 7 = 35$	$6 * 9 = 54$	$30 \div 5 = 6$	$30 \div 10 = 3$
$9 \times 10 = 90$	$10 \times 3 = 30$	$18 / 9 = 2$	$6 / 2 = 3$
$6 \cdot 10 = 60$	$3 \cdot 2 = 6$	$50 \div 10 = 5$	$50 \div 5 = 10$
$8 * 2 = 16$	$5 * 8 = 40$	$14 / 2 = 7$	$27 / 9 = 3$
$5 \times 6 = 30$	$9 \times 9 = 81$	$25 / 5 = 5$	$70 / 10 = 7$
$9 \cdot 5 = 45$	$10 \cdot 4 = 40$	$81 \div 9 = 9$	$20 \div 2 = 10$
$8 * 10 = 80$	$9 * 2 = 18$	$20 / 10 = 2$	$45 / 5 = 9$
$2 \times 1 = 2$	$5 \times 1 = 5$	$8 \div 2 = 4$	$54 \div 9 = 6$
$3 \cdot 5 = 15$	$9 \cdot 6 = 54$	$45 / 5 = 9$	$80 / 10 = 8$
$4 * 9 = 36$	$10 * 1 = 10$	$63 \div 9 = 7$	$16 \div 2 = 8$
$3 \times 10 = 30$	$7 \times 2 = 14$	$30 / 10 = 3$	$15 / 5 = 3$
$2 \cdot 6 = 12$	$6 \cdot 5 = 30$	$10 \div 2 = 5$	$90 \div 9 = 10$
$4 * 5 = 20$	$8 * 9 = 72$	$40 \div 5 = 8$	$100 \div 10 = 10$
$9 \times 7 = 63$	$10 \times 6 = 60$	$9 / 9 = 1$	$12 / 2 = 6$
$1 \cdot 10 = 10$	$2 \cdot 8 = 16$	$50 \div 10 = 5$	$35 \div 5 = 7$

Check Sheet 3: 2s, 5s, 9s, and 10s

Name _____ Date _____

Study Sheet B

4s

Count-bys	Mixed Up ×	Mixed Up ÷
$1 \times 4 = 4$	$4 \times 4 = 16$	$12 \div 4 = 3$
$2 \times 4 = 8$	$1 \times 4 = 4$	$36 \div 4 = 9$
$3 \times 4 = 12$	$7 \times 4 = 28$	$24 \div 4 = 6$
$4 \times 4 = 16$	$3 \times 4 = 12$	$4 \div 4 = 1$
$5 \times 4 = 20$	$9 \times 4 = 36$	$20 \div 4 = 5$
$6 \times 4 = 24$	$10 \times 4 = 40$	$28 \div 4 = 7$
$7 \times 4 = 28$	$2 \times 4 = 8$	$8 \div 4 = 2$
$8 \times 4 = 32$	$5 \times 4 = 20$	$40 \div 4 = 10$
$9 \times 4 = 36$	$8 \times 4 = 32$	$32 \div 4 = 8$
$10 \times 4 = 40$	$6 \times 4 = 24$	$16 \div 4 = 4$

1s

Count-bys	Mixed Up ×	Mixed Up ÷
$1 \times 1 = 1$	$5 \times 1 = 5$	$10 \div 1 = 10$
$2 \times 1 = 2$	$7 \times 1 = 7$	$8 \div 1 = 8$
$3 \times 1 = 3$	$10 \times 1 = 10$	$4 \div 1 = 4$
$4 \times 1 = 4$	$1 \times 1 = 1$	$9 \div 1 = 9$
$5 \times 1 = 5$	$8 \times 1 = 8$	$6 \div 1 = 6$
$6 \times 1 = 6$	$4 \times 1 = 4$	$7 \div 1 = 7$
$7 \times 1 = 7$	$9 \times 1 = 9$	$1 \div 1 = 1$
$8 \times 1 = 8$	$3 \times 1 = 3$	$2 \div 1 = 2$
$9 \times 1 = 9$	$2 \times 1 = 2$	$5 \div 1 = 5$
$10 \times 1 = 10$	$6 \times 1 = 6$	$3 \div 1 = 3$

3s

Count-bys	Mixed Up ×	Mixed Up ÷
$1 \times 3 = 3$	$5 \times 3 = 15$	$27 \div 3 = 9$
$2 \times 3 = 6$	$1 \times 3 = 3$	$6 \div 3 = 2$
$3 \times 3 = 9$	$8 \times 3 = 24$	$18 \div 3 = 6$
$4 \times 3 = 12$	$10 \times 3 = 30$	$30 \div 3 = 10$
$5 \times 3 = 15$	$3 \times 3 = 9$	$9 \div 3 = 3$
$6 \times 3 = 18$	$7 \times 3 = 21$	$3 \div 3 = 1$
$7 \times 3 = 21$	$9 \times 3 = 27$	$12 \div 3 = 4$
$8 \times 3 = 24$	$2 \times 3 = 6$	$24 \div 3 = 8$
$9 \times 3 = 27$	$4 \times 3 = 12$	$15 \div 3 = 5$
$10 \times 3 = 30$	$6 \times 3 = 18$	$21 \div 3 = 7$

0s

Count-bys	Mixed Up ×
$1 \times 0 = 0$	$3 \times 0 = 0$
$2 \times 0 = 0$	$10 \times 0 = 0$
$3 \times 0 = 0$	$5 \times 0 = 0$
$4 \times 0 = 0$	$8 \times 0 = 0$
$5 \times 0 = 0$	$7 \times 0 = 0$
$6 \times 0 = 0$	$2 \times 0 = 0$
$7 \times 0 = 0$	$9 \times 0 = 0$
$8 \times 0 = 0$	$6 \times 0 = 0$
$9 \times 0 = 0$	$1 \times 0 = 0$
$10 \times 0 = 0$	$4 \times 0 = 0$

| 2×2 | $\begin{array}{r} 2 \\ \times 3 \end{array}$ $\begin{array}{r} 3 \\ \times 2 \end{array}$ | 2×4 4×2 | $\begin{array}{r} 2 \\ \times 5 \end{array}$ $\begin{array}{r} 5 \\ \times 2 \end{array}$ |

| 2×6 6×2 | $\begin{array}{r} 2 \\ \times 7 \end{array}$ $\begin{array}{r} 7 \\ \times 2 \end{array}$ | 2×8 8×2 | $\begin{array}{r} 2 \\ \times 9 \end{array}$ $\begin{array}{r} 9 \\ \times 2 \end{array}$ |

Card 1:
$$10 = 2 \times 5$$
$$10 = 5 \times 2$$

5	2
10	4
	6
	8
	10

5
2 ○ ○ ○ ○ ○
○ 10

Card 2:
$$\begin{array}{c} 2 \\ \times 4 \\ \hline 8 \end{array} \qquad \begin{array}{c} 4 \\ \times 2 \\ \hline 8 \end{array}$$

2	4
4	8
6	
8	

2
○ ○
4 ○ 8
○

Card 3:
$$6 = 2 \times 3$$
$$6 = 3 \times 2$$

3	2
6	4
	6

3
2 ○ ○ ○
○ 6

Card 4:
$$\begin{array}{c} 2 \\ \times 2 \\ \hline 4 \end{array}$$

2
4

2
2 ○ ○
○ 4

Card 5:
$$18 = 2 \times 9$$
$$18 = 9 \times 2$$

9	2
18	4
	6
	8
	10
	12
	14
	16
	18

9
2 ○ ○ ○ ○ ○ ○ ○ ○ ○
○ 18

Card 6:
$$\begin{array}{c} 2 \\ \times 8 \\ \hline 16 \end{array} \qquad \begin{array}{c} 8 \\ \times 2 \\ \hline 16 \end{array}$$

2	8
8	16
16	

2
○
○
○
○
8 ○ 16
○
○
○

Card 7:
$$14 = 2 \times 7$$
$$14 = 7 \times 2$$

7	2
14	4
	6
	8
	10
	12
	14

7
2 ○ ○ ○ ○ ○ ○ ○
○ 14

Card 8:
$$\begin{array}{c} 2 \\ \times 6 \\ \hline 12 \end{array} \qquad \begin{array}{c} 6 \\ \times 2 \\ \hline 12 \end{array}$$

2	6
6	12
12	

2
○
○
6 ○ 12
○
○

Multiplication Strategy Cards

| 3×3 | $\begin{array}{r} 3 \\ \times\, 4 \end{array}$ $\begin{array}{r} 4 \\ \times\, 3 \end{array}$ | $\begin{array}{l} 3 \times 5 \\ 5 \times 3 \end{array}$ | $\begin{array}{r} 3 \\ \times\, 6 \end{array}$ $\begin{array}{r} 6 \\ \times\, 3 \end{array}$ |

| $\begin{array}{l} 3 \times 7 \\ 7 \times 3 \end{array}$ | $\begin{array}{r} 3 \\ \times\, 8 \end{array}$ $\begin{array}{r} 8 \\ \times\, 3 \end{array}$ | $\begin{array}{l} 3 \times 9 \\ 9 \times 3 \end{array}$ | $\begin{array}{r} 4 \\ \times\, 4 \end{array}$ |

Card 1

$18 = 3 \times 6$

$18 = 6 \times 3$

6	3
12	6
18	9
	12
	15
	18

6
3○ 18

Card 2

3   5

$\begin{array}{r} \times 5 \\ \hline 15 \end{array}$ $\begin{array}{r} \times 3 \\ \hline 15 \end{array}$

5	3
10	6
15	9
	12
	15

3
5○ 15

Card 3

$12 = 3 \times 4$

$12 = 4 \times 3$

4	3
8	6
12	9
	12

4
3○ 12

Card 4

3

$\begin{array}{r} \times 3 \\ \hline 9 \end{array}$

3
6
9

3
3○ 9

Card 5

$16 = 4 \times 4$

4
8
12
16

4
4○ 16

Card 6

3   9

$\begin{array}{r} \times 9 \\ \hline 27 \end{array}$ $\begin{array}{r} \times 3 \\ \hline 27 \end{array}$

9	3
18	6
27	9
	12
	15
	18
	21
	24
	27

9
3○ 27

Card 7

$24 = 3 \times 8$

$24 = 8 \times 3$

8	3
16	6
24	9
	12
	15
	18
	21
	24

3
8○ 24

Card 8

3   7

$\begin{array}{r} \times 7 \\ \hline 21 \end{array}$ $\begin{array}{r} \times 3 \\ \hline 21 \end{array}$

7	3
14	6
21	9
	12
	15
	18
	21

7
3○ 21

Multiplication Strategy Cards

| 4 × 5 | 4   6 | 4 × 7 | 4   8 |
| 5 × 4 | × 6   × 4 | 7 × 4 | × 8   × 4 |

| 4 × 9 | 5 | 5 × 6 | 5   7 |
| 9 × 4 | × 5 | 6 × 5 | × 7   × 5 |

Card 1

$32 = 4 \times 8$

$32 = 8 \times 4$

8	4
16	8
24	12
32	16
	20
	24
	28
	32

4

8 32

Card 2

$\begin{array}{r} 4 \\ \times 7 \\ \hline 28 \end{array}$ $\begin{array}{r} 7 \\ \times 4 \\ \hline 28 \end{array}$

7	4
14	8
21	12
28	16
	20
	24
	28

7

4 28

Card 3

$24 = 4 \times 6$

$24 = 6 \times 4$

6	4
12	8
18	12
24	16
	20
	24

4

6 24

Card 4

$\begin{array}{r} 4 \\ \times 5 \\ \hline 20 \end{array}$ $\begin{array}{r} 5 \\ \times 4 \\ \hline 20 \end{array}$

5	4
10	8
15	12
20	16
	20

5

4 20

Card 5

$35 = 5 \times 7$

$35 = 7 \times 5$

7	5
14	10
21	15
28	20
35	25
	30
	35

7

5 35

Card 6

$\begin{array}{r} 5 \\ \times 6 \\ \hline 30 \end{array}$ $\begin{array}{r} 6 \\ \times 5 \\ \hline 30 \end{array}$

6	5
12	10
18	15
24	20
30	25
	30

5

6 30

Card 7

$25 = 5 \times 5$

5
10
15
20
25

5

5 25

Card 8

$\begin{array}{r} 4 \\ \times 9 \\ \hline 36 \end{array}$ $\begin{array}{r} 9 \\ \times 4 \\ \hline 36 \end{array}$

9	4
18	8
27	12
36	16
	20
	24
	28
	32
	36

9

4 36

Multiplication Strategy Cards

5×8
8×5

$\begin{array}{r} 5 \\ \times 9 \end{array}$ $\begin{array}{r} 9 \\ \times 5 \end{array}$

6×6

$\begin{array}{r} 6 \\ \times 7 \end{array}$ $\begin{array}{r} 7 \\ \times 6 \end{array}$

6×8
8×6

$\begin{array}{r} 6 \\ \times 9 \end{array}$ $\begin{array}{r} 9 \\ \times 6 \end{array}$

7×7

$\begin{array}{r} 7 \\ \times 8 \end{array}$ $\begin{array}{r} 8 \\ \times 7 \end{array}$

Card 1

$42 = 7 \times 6$

$42 = 6 \times 7$

6	7
12	14
18	21
24	28
30	35
36	42
42	

7

6 | 42

Card 2

$\times\ 6$ over 6

36

6
12
18
24
30
36

6

6 | 36

Card 3

$45 = 9 \times 5$

$45 = 5 \times 9$

5	9
10	18
15	27
20	36
25	45
30	
35	
40	
45	

9

5 | 45

Card 4

8   5
$\times\ 5$ $\times\ 8$
40   40

5	8
10	16
15	24
20	32
25	40
30	
35	
40	

5

8 | 40

Card 5

$56 = 7 \times 8$

$56 = 8 \times 7$

8	7
16	14
24	21
32	28
40	35
48	42
56	49
	56

8

7 | 56

Card 6

7
$\times\ 7$
49

7
14
21
28
35
42
49

7

7 | 49

Card 7

$54 = 9 \times 6$

$54 = 6 \times 9$

6	9
12	18
18	27
24	36
30	45
36	54
42	
48	
54	

9

6 | 54

Card 8

6   8
$\times\ 8$ $\times\ 6$
48   48

6	8
12	16
18	24
24	32
30	40
36	48
42	
48	

8

6 | 48

Multiplication Strategy Cards

7×9
9×7

$\begin{array}{r} 8 \\ \times\ 8 \\ \hline \end{array}$

9×8
8×9

$\begin{array}{r} 9 \\ \times\ 9 \\ \hline \end{array}$

81 = 9 × 9

9
18
27
36
45

54
63
72
81

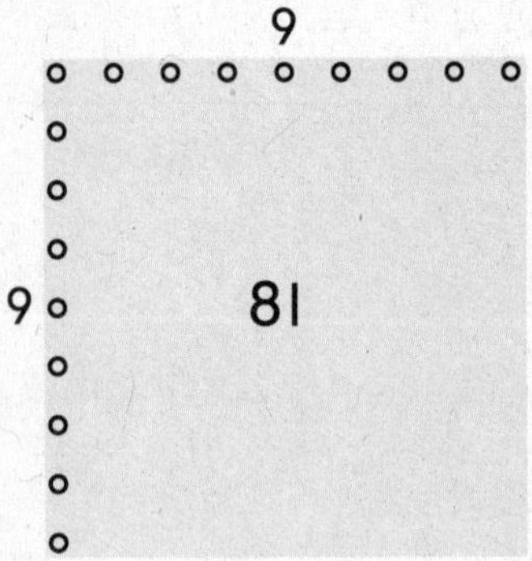

9	8
× 8	× 9
72	72

8	9
16	18
24	27
32	36
40	45
48	54
56	63
64	72
72	

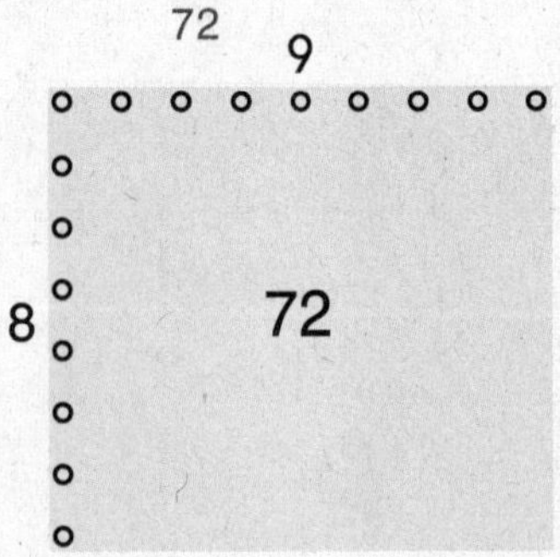

64 = 8 × 8

8
16
24
32
40

48
56
64

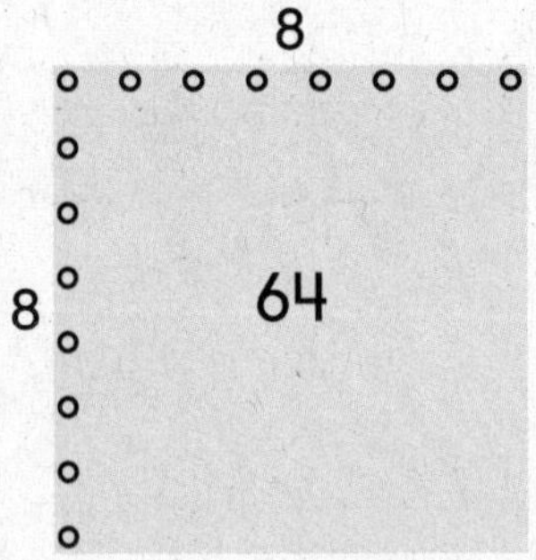

7	9
× 9	× 7
63	63

9	7
18	14
27	21
36	28
45	35
54	42
63	49
	56
	63

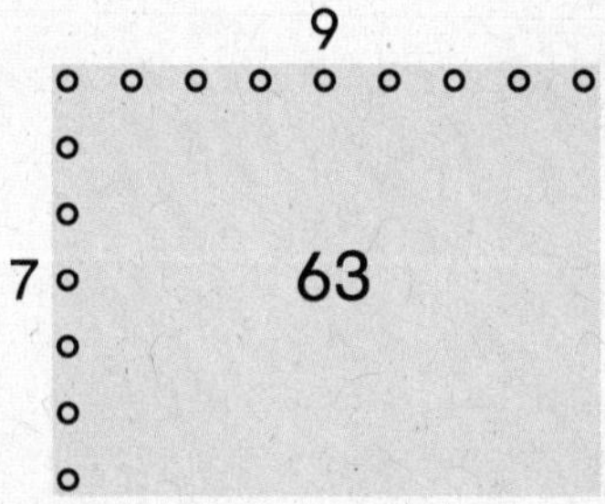

$2\overline{)4}$

$4 \div 2$

$2\overline{)6}$

$6 \div 2$

$2\overline{)8}$

$8 \div 2$

$2\overline{)10}$

$10 \div 2$

$2\overline{)12}$

$12 \div 2$

$2\overline{)14}$

$14 \div 2$

$2\overline{)16}$

$16 \div 2$

$2\overline{)18}$

$18 \div 2$

$$2\overline{)10} \quad 5\overline{)10}$$

2	5
4	10
6	
8	
10	

5

2 · · · · ·
2 · **10**

$$2\overline{)8} \quad 4\overline{)8}$$

2	4
4	8
6	
8	

4

2 · · · ·
2 · **8**

$$2\overline{)6} \quad 3\overline{)6}$$

2	3
4	6
6	

3

2 · · ·
2 · **6**

$$2\overline{)4}$$

2
4

2

2 · ·
2 · **4**

$$2\overline{)18} \quad 9\overline{)18}$$

2	9
4	18
6	
8	
10	
12	
14	
16	
18	

9

2 · · · · · · · · ·
2 · **18**

$$2\overline{)16} \quad 8\overline{)16}$$

2	8
4	16
6	
8	
10	
12	
14	
16	

8

2 · · · · · · · ·
2 · **16**

$$2\overline{)14} \quad 7\overline{)14}$$

2	7
4	14
6	
8	
10	
12	
14	

7

2 · · · · · · ·
2 · **14**

$$2\overline{)12} \quad 6\overline{)12}$$

2	6
4	12
6	
8	
10	
12	

6

2 · · · · · ·
2 · **12**

Division Strategy Cards

$3 \overline{)6}$	$4 \overline{)8}$	$5 \overline{)10}$	$6 \overline{)12}$
$6 \div 3$	$8 \div 4$	$10 \div 5$	$12 \div 6$

$7 \overline{)14}$	$8 \overline{)16}$	$9 \overline{)18}$	$3 \overline{)9}$
$14 \div 7$	$16 \div 8$	$18 \div 9$	$9 \div 3$

Row 1

$$6\overline{)12} \quad \quad 2\overline{)12}$$
2 → 2
6 12 → 4
     6
     8
     10
     12

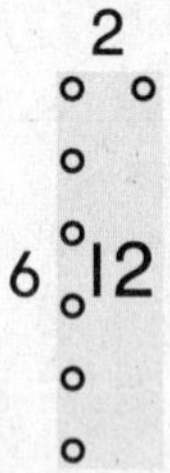

$$5\overline{)10} \quad \quad 2\overline{)10}$$
5 → 2
10 → 4
     6
     8
     10

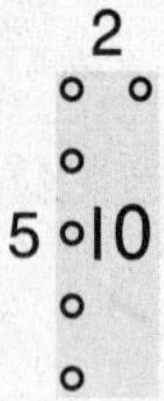

$$4\overline{)8} \quad \quad 2\overline{)8}$$
4 → 2
8 → 4
     6
     8

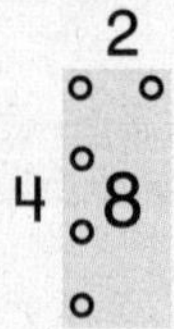

$$3\overline{)6} \quad \quad 2\overline{)6}$$
3 → 2
6 → 4
    6

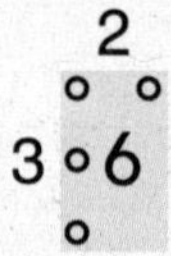

2
6 ○ 12

2
5 ○ 10

2
4 ○ 8

2
3 ○ 6

Row 2

$$3\overline{)9}$$
3
6
9

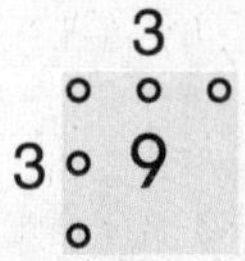

$$9\overline{)18} \quad \quad 2\overline{)18}$$
9 → 2
18 → 4
     6
     8
     10
     12
     14
     16
     18

$$8\overline{)16} \quad \quad 2\overline{)16}$$
8 → 2
16 → 4
     6
     8
     10
     12
     14
     16

$$7\overline{)14} \quad \quad 2\overline{)14}$$
7 → 2
14 → 4
     6
     8
     10
     12
     14

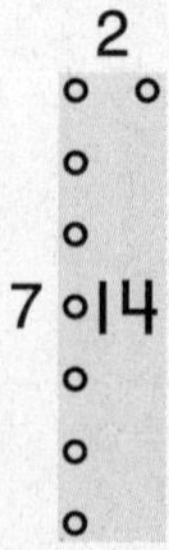

3
3 ○ 9

2
9 ○ 18

2
8 ○ 16

2
7 ○ 14

Division Strategy Cards

$3\overline{)12}$
$12 \div 3$

$3\overline{)15}$
$15 \div 3$

$3\overline{)18}$
$18 \div 3$

$3\overline{)21}$
$21 \div 3$

$3\overline{)24}$
$24 \div 3$

$3\overline{)27}$
$27 \div 3$

$4\overline{)12}$
$12 \div 4$

$5\overline{)15}$
$15 \div 5$

Card 1

$$7 \quad\quad 3$$
$$3\overline{)21} \quad 7\overline{)21}$$

3	7
6	14
9	21
12	
15	
18	
21	

7
3 · 21

Card 2

$$6 \quad\quad 3$$
$$3\overline{)18} \quad 6\overline{)18}$$

3	6
6	12
9	18
12	
15	
18	

6
3 · 18

Card 3

$$5 \quad\quad 3$$
$$3\overline{)15} \quad 5\overline{)15}$$

3	5
6	10
9	15
12	
15	

5
3 · 15

Card 4

$$4 \quad\quad 3$$
$$3\overline{)12} \quad 4\overline{)12}$$

3	4
6	8
9	12
12	

4
3 · 12

Card 5

$$3 \quad\quad 5$$
$$5\overline{)15} \quad 3\overline{)15}$$

5	3
10	6
15	9
	12
	15

3
5 · 15

Card 6

$$3 \quad\quad 4$$
$$4\overline{)12} \quad 3\overline{)12}$$

4	3
8	6
12	9
	12

3
4 · 12

Card 7

$$9 \quad\quad 3$$
$$3\overline{)27} \quad 9\overline{)27}$$

3	9
6	18
9	27
12	
15	
18	
21	
24	
27	

9
3 · 27

Card 8

$$8 \quad\quad 3$$
$$3\overline{)24} \quad 8\overline{)24}$$

3	8
6	16
9	24
12	
15	
18	
21	
24	

8
3 · 24

Division Strategy Cards

$6\overline{)18}$	$7\overline{)21}$	$8\overline{)24}$	$9\overline{)27}$
$18 \div 6$	$21 \div 7$	$24 \div 8$	$27 \div 9$

$4\overline{)16}$	$4\overline{)20}$	$4\overline{)24}$	$4\overline{)28}$
$16 \div 4$	$20 \div 4$	$24 \div 4$	$28 \div 4$

Card 1

$$3$$
$$9\overline{)27}$$ $$3\overline{)27}$$

9	3
18	6
27	9
	12
	15
	18
	21
	24
	27

3

9 27

Card 2

$$3$$ $$8$$
$$8\overline{)24}$$ $$3\overline{)24}$$

8	3
16	6
24	9
	12
	15
	18
	21
	24

3

8 24

Card 3

$$3$$ $$7$$
$$7\overline{)21}$$ $$3\overline{)21}$$

7	3
14	6
21	9
	12
	15
	18
	21

3

7 21

Card 4

$$3$$ $$6$$
$$6\overline{)18}$$ $$3\overline{)18}$$

6	3
12	6
18	9
	12
	15
	18

3

6 18

Card 5

$$7$$ $$4$$
$$4\overline{)28}$$ $$7\overline{)28}$$

4	7
8	14
12	21
16	28
20	
24	
28	

7

4 28

Card 6

$$6$$ $$4$$
$$4\overline{)24}$$ $$6\overline{)24}$$

4	6
8	12
12	18
16	24
20	
24	

6

4 24

Card 7

$$5$$ $$4$$
$$4\overline{)20}$$ $$5\overline{)20}$$

4	5
8	10
12	15
16	20
20	

5

4 20

Card 8

$$4$$
$$4\overline{)16}$$

4
8
12
16

4

4 16

Division Strategy Cards

$4 \overline{)32}$

$32 \div 4$

$4 \overline{)36}$

$36 \div 4$

$5 \overline{)20}$

$20 \div 5$

$6 \overline{)24}$

$24 \div 6$

$7 \overline{)28}$

$28 \div 7$

$8 \overline{)32}$

$32 \div 8$

$9 \overline{)36}$

$36 \div 9$

$5 \overline{)25}$

$25 \div 5$

Card 1

$$4 \qquad 6$$
$$6\overline{)24} \quad 4\overline{)24}$$

6	4
12	8
18	12
24	16
	20
	24

4
6 · 24

Card 2

$$4 \qquad 5$$
$$5\overline{)20} \quad 4\overline{)20}$$

5	4
10	8
15	12
20	16
	20

4
5 · 20

Card 3

$$9 \qquad 4$$
$$4\overline{)36} \quad 9\overline{)36}$$

4	9
8	18
12	27
16	36
20	
24	
28	
32	
36	

9
4 · 36

Card 4

$$8 \qquad 4$$
$$4\overline{)32} \quad 8\overline{)32}$$

4	8
8	16
12	24
16	32
20	
24	
28	
32	

8
4 · 32

Card 5

$$5$$
$$5\overline{)25}$$

5
10
15
20
25

5
5 · 25

Card 6

$$4 \qquad 9$$
$$9\overline{)36} \quad 4\overline{)36}$$

9	4
18	8
27	12
36	16
	20
	24
	28
	32
	36

4
9 · 36

Card 7

$$4 \qquad 8$$
$$8\overline{)32} \quad 4\overline{)32}$$

8	4
16	8
24	12
32	16
	20
	24
	28
	32

4
8 · 32

Card 8

$$4 \qquad 7$$
$$7\overline{)28} \quad 4\overline{)28}$$

7	4
14	8
21	12
28	16
	20
	24
	28

4
7 · 28

Division Strategy Cards

| $5\overline{)30}$ | $5\overline{)35}$ | $5\overline{)40}$ | $5\overline{)45}$ |
| $30 \div 5$ | $35 \div 5$ | $40 \div 5$ | $45 \div 5$ |

| $6\overline{)30}$ | $7\overline{)35}$ | $8\overline{)40}$ | $9\overline{)45}$ |
| $30 \div 6$ | $35 \div 7$ | $40 \div 8$ | $45 \div 9$ |

Division Strategy Cards — Unit 1 Lesson 11

9 $5\overline{)45}$	5 $9\overline{)45}$	8 $5\overline{)40}$	5 $8\overline{)40}$	7 $5\overline{)35}$	5 $7\overline{)35}$	6 $5\overline{)30}$	5 $6\overline{)30}$
5 10 15 20 25 30 35 40 45	9 18 27 36 45	5 10 15 20 25 30 35 40	8 16 24 32 40	5 10 15 20 25 30 35	7 14 21 28 35	5 10 15 20 25 30	6 12 18 24 30

Card 1: 9 across / 5 down — 45

Card 2: 8 across / 5 down — 40

Card 3: 7 across / 5 down — 35

Card 4: 6 across / 5 down — 30

5 $9\overline{)45}$	9 $5\overline{)45}$	5 $8\overline{)40}$	8 $5\overline{)40}$	5 $7\overline{)35}$	7 $5\overline{)35}$	5 $6\overline{)30}$	6 $5\overline{)30}$
9 18 27 36 45	5 10 15 20 25 30 35 40 45	8 16 24 32 40	5 10 15 20 25 30 35 40	7 14 21 28 35	5 10 15 20 25 30 35	6 12 18 24 30	5 10 15 20 25 30

Card 5: 5 across / 9 down — 45

Card 6: 5 across / 8 down — 40

Card 7: 5 across / 7 down — 35

Card 8: 5 across / 6 down — 30

Division Strategy Cards

$6 \overline{)36}$

$36 \div 6$

$6 \overline{)42}$

$42 \div 6$

$6 \overline{)48}$

$48 \div 6$

$6 \overline{)54}$

$54 \div 6$

$7 \overline{)42}$

$42 \div 7$

$8 \overline{)48}$

$48 \div 8$

$9 \overline{)54}$

$54 \div 9$

$7 \overline{)49}$

$49 \div 7$

Card 1

$6\overline{)54}$ $\quad$ $9\overline{)54}$

6	9
12	18
18	27
24	36
30	45
36	54
42	
48	
54	

9

6 — 54

Card 2

$6\overline{)48}$ $\quad$ $8\overline{)48}$

6	8
12	16
18	24
24	32
30	40
36	48
42	
48	

8

6 — 48

Card 3

$6\overline{)42}$ $\quad$ $7\overline{)42}$

6	7
12	14
18	21
24	28
30	35
36	42
42	

7

6 — 42

Card 4

$6\overline{)36}$

6
12
18
24
30
36

6

6 — 36

Card 5

$7\overline{)49}$

7
14
21
28
35
42
49

7

7 — 49

Card 6

$9\overline{)54}$ $\quad$ $6\overline{)54}$

9	6
18	12
27	18
36	24
45	30
54	36
	42
	48
	54

6

9 — 54

Card 7

$8\overline{)48}$ $\quad$ $6\overline{)48}$

8	6
16	12
24	18
32	24
40	30
48	36
	42
	48

6

8 — 48

Card 8

$7\overline{)42}$ $\quad$ $6\overline{)42}$

7	6
14	12
21	18
28	24
35	30
42	36
	42

6

7 — 42

Division Strategy Cards

$7 \overline{)56}$

$56 \div 7$

$7 \overline{)63}$

$63 \div 7$

$8 \overline{)56}$

$56 \div 8$

$9 \overline{)63}$

$63 \div 9$

$8 \overline{)64}$

$64 \div 8$

$8 \overline{)72}$

$72 \div 8$

$9 \overline{)72}$

$72 \div 9$

$9 \overline{)81}$

$81 \div 9$

Card 1

$$7 \quad 9$$
$$9\overline{)63} \quad 7\overline{)63}$$

9	7
18	14
27	21
36	28
45	35
54	42
63	49
	56
	63

7

9) 63

Card 2

$$7 \quad 8$$
$$8\overline{)56} \quad 7\overline{)56}$$

8	7
16	14
24	21
32	28
40	35
48	42
56	49
	56

7

8) 56

Card 3

$$9 \quad 7$$
$$7\overline{)63} \quad 9\overline{)63}$$

7	9
14	18
21	27
28	36
35	45
42	54
49	63
56	
63	

9

7) 63

Card 4

$$8 \quad 7$$
$$7\overline{)56} \quad 8\overline{)56}$$

7	8
14	16
21	24
28	32
35	40
42	48
49	56
56	

8

7) 56

Card 5

$$9$$
$$9\overline{)81}$$

9
18
27
36
45
54
63
72
81

9

9) 81

Card 6

$$8 \quad 9$$
$$9\overline{)72} \quad 8\overline{)72}$$

9	8
18	16
27	24
36	32
45	40
54	48
63	56
72	64
	72

8

9) 72

Card 7

$$9 \quad 8$$
$$8\overline{)72} \quad 9\overline{)72}$$

8	9
16	18
24	27
32	36
40	45
48	54
56	63
64	7.2
72	

9

8) 72

Card 8

$$8$$
$$8\overline{)64}$$

8
16
24
32
40
48
56
64

8

8) 64

Division Strategy Cards

▶ **PATH to FLUENCY** **Check Sheet 4: 3s and 4s**

3s Multiplications	3s Divisions	4s Multiplications	4s Divisions
$8 \times 3 = 24$	$9 / 3 = 3$	$1 \times 4 = 4$	$40 / 4 = 10$
$3 \cdot 2 = 6$	$21 \div 3 = 7$	$4 \cdot 5 = 20$	$12 \div 4 = 3$
$3 * 5 = 15$	$27 / 3 = 9$	$8 * 4 = 32$	$24 / 4 = 6$
$10 \times 3 = 30$	$3 \div 3 = 1$	$3 \times 4 = 12$	$8 \div 4 = 2$
$3 \cdot 3 = 9$	$18 / 3 = 6$	$4 \cdot 6 = 24$	$4 / 4 = 1$
$3 * 6 = 18$	$12 \div 3 = 4$	$4 * 9 = 36$	$28 \div 4 = 7$
$7 \times 3 = 21$	$30 / 3 = 10$	$10 \times 4 = 40$	$32 / 4 = 8$
$3 \cdot 9 = 27$	$6 \div 3 = 2$	$4 \cdot 7 = 28$	$16 \div 4 = 4$
$4 * 3 = 12$	$24 / 3 = 8$	$4 * 4 = 16$	$36 / 4 = 9$
$3 \times 1 = 3$	$15 / 3 = 5$	$2 \times 4 = 8$	$20 / 4 = 5$
$3 \cdot 4 = 12$	$21 \div 3 = 7$	$4 \cdot 3 = 12$	$4 \div 4 = 1$
$3 * 3 = 9$	$3 / 3 = 1$	$4 * 2 = 8$	$32 / 4 = 8$
$3 \times 10 = 30$	$9 \div 3 = 3$	$9 \times 4 = 36$	$8 \div 4 = 2$
$2 \cdot 3 = 6$	$27 / 3 = 9$	$1 \cdot 4 = 4$	$16 / 4 = 4$
$3 * 7 = 21$	$30 \div 3 = 10$	$4 * 6 = 24$	$36 \div 4 = 9$
$6 \times 3 = 18$	$18 / 3 = 6$	$5 \times 4 = 20$	$12 / 4 = 3$
$5 \cdot 3 = 15$	$6 \div 3 = 2$	$4 \cdot 4 = 16$	$40 \div 4 = 10$
$3 * 8 = 24$	$15 \div 3 = 5$	$7 * 4 = 28$	$20 \div 4 = 5$
$9 \times 3 = 27$	$12 / 3 = 4$	$8 \times 4 = 32$	$24 / 4 = 6$
$2 \cdot 3 = 6$	$24 \div 3 = 8$	$10 \cdot 4 = 40$	$28 \div 4 = 7$

▶ PATH to FLUENCY **Play *Solve the Stack***

Read the rules for playing *Solve the Stack*. Then play the game with your group.

> **Rules for *Solve the Stack***
>
> *Number of players:* 2–4
>
> *What you will need:* 1 set of multiplication and division Strategy Cards
>
> 1. Shuffle the cards. Place them exercise side up in the center of the table.
> 2. Players take turns. On each turn, a player finds the answer to the multiplication or division on the top card and then turns the card over to check the answer.
> 3. If a player's answer is correct, he or she takes the card. If it is incorrect, the card is placed at the bottom of the stack.
> 4. Play ends when there are no more cards in the stack. The player with the most cards wins.

► (PATH to FLUENCY) Play *High Card Wins*

Read the rules for playing *High Card Wins*. Then play the game with your partner.

Rules for *High Card Wins*

Number of players: 2

What you will need: 1 set of multiplication and division Strategy Cards for 2s, 3s, 4s, 5s, 9s

1. Shuffle the cards. Deal all the cards evenly between the two players.

2. Players put their stacks in front of them, exercise side up.

3. Each player takes the top card from his or her stack and puts it exercise side up in the center of the table.

4. Each player says the multiplication or division answer and then turns the card over to check. Then players do one of the following:

   • If one player says the wrong answer, the other player takes both cards and puts them at the bottom of his or her pile.

   • If both players say the wrong answer, both players take back their cards and put them at the bottom of their piles.

   • If both players say the correct answer, the player with the higher product or quotient takes both cards and puts them at the bottom of his or her pile. If the products or quotients are the same, the players set the cards aside and play another round. The winner of the next round takes all the cards.

5. Play continues until one player has all the cards.

Use the Strategy Cards

Name   Date

► PATH to FLUENCY **Check Sheet 5: 1s and 0s**

1s Multiplications	1s Divisions	0s Multiplications
$1 \times 4 = 4$	$10 / 1 = 10$	$4 \times 0 = 0$
$5 \cdot 1 = 5$	$5 \div 1 = 5$	$2 \cdot 0 = 0$
$7 * 1 = 7$	$7 / 1 = 7$	$0 * 8 = 0$
$1 \times 8 = 8$	$9 \div 1 = 9$	$0 \times 5 = 0$
$1 \cdot 6 = 6$	$3 / 1 = 3$	$6 \cdot 0 = 0$
$10 * 1 = 10$	$10 \div 1 = 10$	$0 * 7 = 0$
$1 \times 9 = 9$	$2 / 1 = 2$	$0 \times 2 = 0$
$3 \cdot 1 = 3$	$8 \div 1 = 8$	$0 \cdot 9 = 0$
$1 * 2 = 2$	$6 / 1 = 6$	$10 * 0 = 0$
$1 \times 1 = 1$	$9 / 1 = 9$	$1 \times 0 = 0$
$8 \cdot 1 = 8$	$1 \div 1 = 1$	$0 \cdot 6 = 0$
$1 * 7 = 7$	$5 / 1 = 5$	$9 * 0 = 0$
$1 \times 5 = 5$	$3 \div 1 = 3$	$0 \times 4 = 0$
$6 \cdot 1 = 6$	$4 / 1 = 4$	$3 \cdot 0 = 0$
$1 * 1 = 1$	$2 \div 1 = 2$	$0 * 3 = 0$
$1 \times 10 = 10$	$8 / 1 = 8$	$8 \times 0 = 0$
$9 \cdot 1 = 9$	$4 \div 1 = 4$	$0 \cdot 10 = 0$
$4 * 1 = 4$	$7 \div 1 = 7$	$0 * 1 = 0$
$2 \times 1 = 2$	$1 / 1 = 1$	$5 \times 0 = 0$
$1 \cdot 3 = 3$	$6 \div 1 = 6$	$7 \cdot 0 = 0$

Name _____ Date _____

► **PATH to FLUENCY** **Check Sheet 6: Mixed 3s, 4s, 0s, and 1s**

3s, 4s, 0s, 1s Multiplications	3s, 4s, 0s, 1s Multiplications	3s, 4s, 1s Divisions	3s, 4s, 1s Divisions
5 × 3 = 15	0 × 5 = 0	18 / 3 = 6	4 / 1 = 4
6 • 4 = 24	10 • 1 = 10	20 ÷ 4 = 5	21 ÷ 3 = 7
9 * 0 = 0	6 * 3 = 18	1 / 1 = 1	16 / 4 = 4
7 × 1 = 7	2 × 4 = 8	21 ÷ 3 = 7	9 ÷ 1 = 9
3 • 3 = 9	5 • 0 = 0	12 / 4 = 3	15 / 3 = 5
4 * 7 = 28	1 * 2 = 2	5 ÷ 1 = 5	8 ÷ 4 = 2
0 × 10 = 0	10 × 3 = 30	15 / 3 = 5	5 / 1 = 5
1 • 6 = 6	5 • 4 = 20	24 ÷ 4 = 6	30 ÷ 3 = 10
3 * 4 = 12	0 * 8 = 0	7 / 1 = 7	12 / 4 = 3
5 × 4 = 20	9 × 2 = 18	12 / 3 = 4	8 / 1 = 8
0 • 5 = 0	10 • 3 = 30	36 ÷ 4 = 9	27 ÷ 3 = 9
9 * 1 = 9	9 * 4 = 36	6 / 1 = 6	40 / 4 = 10
2 × 3 = 6	1 × 0 = 0	12 ÷ 3 = 4	4 ÷ 1 = 4
3 • 4 = 12	1 • 6 = 6	16 / 4 = 4	9 / 3 = 3
0 * 9 = 0	3 * 6 = 18	7 ÷ 1 = 7	16 ÷ 4 = 4
1 × 5 = 5	7 × 4 = 28	9 / 3 = 3	10 / 1 = 10
2 • 3 = 6	6 • 0 = 0	8 ÷ 4 = 2	9 ÷ 3 = 3
4 * 4 = 16	8 * 1 = 8	2 ÷ 1 = 2	20 ÷ 4 = 5
9 × 0 = 0	3 × 9 = 27	6 / 3 = 2	6 / 1 = 6
1 • 1 = 1	1 • 4 = 4	32 ÷ 4 = 8	24 ÷ 3 = 8

► PATH to FLUENCY **Play** *Multiplication Three-in-a-Row*

Read the rules for playing *Multiplication Three-in-a-Row*.
Then play the game with a partner.

Rules for *Multiplication Three-in-a-Row*

Number of players: 2

What You Will Need: A set of multiplication Strategy
Cards, *Three-in-a-Row* Game Grids for each player
(see page 75)

1. Each player looks through the cards and writes
   any nine of the products in the squares of a Game
   Grid. A player may write the same product more
   than once.

2. Shuffle the cards and place them exercise side up
   in the center of the table.

3. Players take turns. On each turn, a player finds the
   answer to the multiplication on the top card and
   then turns the card over to check the answer.

4. If the answer is correct, the player looks to see if
   the product is on the game grid. If it is, the player
   puts an X through that grid square. If the answer
   is wrong, or if the product is not on the grid, the
   player does not mark anything. The player then
   puts the card problem side up on the bottom of
   the stack.

5. The first player to mark three squares in a row
   (horizontally, vertically, or diagonally) wins.

► (PATH to FLUENCY) Play *Division Race*

Read the rules for playing *Division Race*. Then play the game with a partner.

Rules for *Division Race*

Number of players: 2

What You Will Need: a set of division Strategy Cards, the *Division Race* game board (see page 76), a different game piece for each player

1. Shuffle the cards and then place them exercise side up on the table.

2. Both players put their game pieces on "START."

3. Players take turns. On each turn, a player finds the answer to the division on the top card and then turns the card over to check the answer.

4. If the answer is correct, the player moves *forward* that number of spaces. If a player's answer is wrong, the player moves *back* a number of spaces equal to the correct answer. Players cannot move back beyond the "START" square. The player puts the card on the bottom of the stack.

5. If a player lands on a space with special instructions, he or she should follow those instructions.

6. The game ends when everyone lands on or passes the "End" square.

Name Date

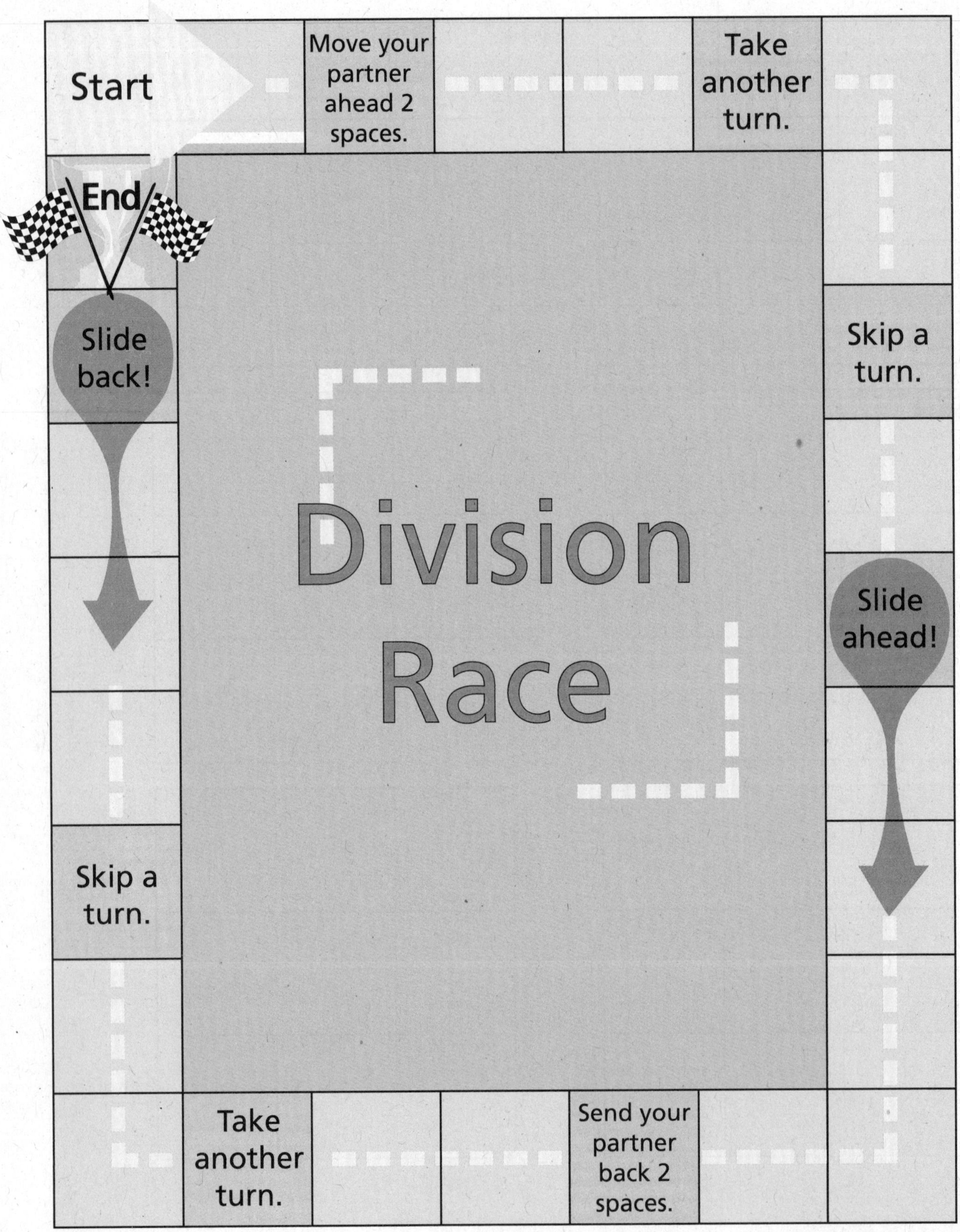
Start
Move your partner ahead 2 spaces.
Take another turn.
Skip a turn.
Slide ahead!
Send your partner back 2 spaces.
Take another turn.
Skip a turn.
Slide back!
End
Division Race

▶ **PATH to FLUENCY** Dashes 1–4

Complete each Dash. Check your answers on page 81.

Dash 1 2s and 5s Multiplications	Dash 2 2s and 5s Divisions	Dash 3 9s and 10s Multiplications	Dash 4 9s and 10s Divisions
a. $2 \times 6 = $ ___	a. $18 / 2 = $ ___	a. $9 \times 10 = $ ___	a. $100 / 10 = $ ___
b. $9 * 5 = $ ___	b. $25 \div 5 = $ ___	b. $10 * 3 = $ ___	b. $9 \div 9 = $ ___
c. $7 \cdot 2 = $ ___	c. $8 / 2 = $ ___	c. $1 \cdot 9 = $ ___	c. $30 / 10 = $ ___
d. $5 \times 8 = $ ___	d. $45 \div 5 = $ ___	d. $2 \times 10 = $ ___	d. $81 \div 9 = $ ___
e. $2 * 4 = $ ___	e. $16 / 2 = $ ___	e. $9 * 9 = $ ___	e. $70 / 10 = $ ___
f. $3 \cdot 5 = $ ___	f. $20 \div 5 = $ ___	f. $10 \cdot 6 = $ ___	f. $45 \div 9 = $ ___
g. $1 \times 2 = $ ___	g. $4 / 2 = $ ___	g. $4 \times 9 = $ ___	g. $10 / 10 = $ ___
h. $5 * 7 = $ ___	h. $40 \div 5 = $ ___	h. $10 \times 10 = $ ___	h. $54 \div 9 = $ ___
i. $2 \cdot 9 = $ ___	i. $20 / 2 = $ ___	i. $9 * 2 = $ ___	i. $50 / 10 = $ ___
j. $4 \times 5 = $ ___	j. $35 \div 5 = $ ___	j. $1 \cdot 10 = $ ___	j. $27 \div 9 = $ ___
k. $5 * 2 = $ ___	k. $6 / 2 = $ ___	k. $7 \times 9 = $ ___	k. $20 / 10 = $ ___
l. $5 \cdot 1 = $ ___	l. $15 \div 5 = $ ___	l. $10 * 5 = $ ___	l. $72 \div 9 = $ ___
m. $2 \times 2 = $ ___	m. $14 / 2 = $ ___	m. $9 \cdot 8 = $ ___	m. $40 / 10 = $ ___
n. $10 \times 5 = $ ___	n. $5 \div 5 = $ ___	n. $7 \times 10 = $ ___	n. $18 \div 9 = $ ___
o. $10 * 2 = $ ___	o. $10 / 2 = $ ___	o. $3 * 9 = $ ___	o. $60 / 10 = $ ___
p. $5 \cdot 6 = $ ___	p. $10 \div 5 = $ ___	p. $10 \cdot 4 = $ ___	p. $90 \div 9 = $ ___
q. $2 \times 3 = $ ___	q. $6 / 2 = $ ___	q. $9 \times 5 = $ ___	q. $90 / 10 = $ ___
r. $5 * 5 = $ ___	r. $30 \div 5 = $ ___	r. $8 * 10 = $ ___	r. $63 \div 9 = $ ___
s. $8 \cdot 2 = $ ___	s. $2 / 2 = $ ___	s. $6 \cdot 9 = $ ___	s. $80 / 10 = $ ___
t. $6 \times 5 = $ ___	t. $45 \div 5 = $ ___	t. $10 \times 9 = $ ___	t. $36 \div 9 = $ ___

► PATH to FLUENCY **Dashes 5–8**

Complete each Dash. Check your answers on page 81.

Dash 5 3s and 4s Multiplications	Dash 6 3s and 4s Divisions	Dash 7 0s and 1s Multiplications	Dash 8 1s and $n \div n$ Divisions
a. $3 \times 9 =$ ___	a. $12 / 4 =$ ___	a. $0 \times 6 =$ ___	a. $9 / 9 =$ ___
b. $4 * 2 =$ ___	b. $20 \div 4 =$ ___	b. $1 * 4 =$ ___	b. $8 \div 1 =$ ___
c. $6 \cdot 3 =$ ___	c. $21 / 3 =$ ___	c. $4 \cdot 0 =$ ___	c. $7 / 7 =$ ___
d. $10 \times 4 =$ ___	d. $16 \div 4 =$ ___	d. $8 \times 1 =$ ___	d. $6 \div 1 =$ ___
e. $3 * 1 =$ ___	e. $9 / 3 =$ ___	e. $0 * 2 =$ ___	e. $1 / 1 =$ ___
f. $4 \cdot 1 =$ ___	f. $32 \div 4 =$ ___	f. $1 \cdot 3 =$ ___	f. $4 \div 1 =$ ___
g. $10 \times 3 =$ ___	g. $24 / 4 =$ ___	g. $9 \times 0 =$ ___	g. $2 / 2 =$ ___
h. $5 * 4 =$ ___	h. $18 \div 3 =$ ___	h. $2 * 1 =$ ___	h. $2 \div 1 =$ ___
i. $3 \cdot 3 =$ ___	i. $40 / 4 =$ ___	i. $0 \cdot 8 =$ ___	i. $8 / 8 =$ ___
j. $4 \times 4 =$ ___	j. $12 \div 3 =$ ___	j. $1 \times 10 =$ ___	j. $9 \div 1 =$ ___
k. $8 * 3 =$ ___	k. $6 / 3 =$ ___	k. $7 * 0 =$ ___	k. $3 / 3 =$ ___
l. $7 \cdot 4 =$ ___	l. $28 \div 4 =$ ___	l. $1 \cdot 1 =$ ___	l. $5 \div 1 =$ ___
m. $3 \times 2 =$ ___	m. $24 / 3 =$ ___	m. $0 \times 0 =$ ___	m. $5 / 5 =$ ___
n. $4 * 9 =$ ___	n. $20 \div 4 =$ ___	n. $5 * 1 =$ ___	n. $10 / 10 =$ ___
o. $7 \cdot 3 =$ ___	o. $27 / 3 =$ ___	o. $1 \cdot 0 =$ ___	o. $7 \div 1 =$ ___
p. $3 \times 4 =$ ___	p. $15 \div 3 =$ ___	p. $1 \times 6 =$ ___	p. $4 / 4 =$ ___
q. $3 * 5 =$ ___	q. $27 / 3 =$ ___	q. $5 * 0 =$ ___	q. $10 \div 1 =$ ___
r. $4 \cdot 6 =$ ___	r. $36 \div 4 =$ ___	r. $0 \cdot 3 =$ ___	r. $6 / 6 =$ ___
s. $4 \times 3 =$ ___	s. $8 / 4 =$ ___	s. $7 \times 1 =$ ___	s. $3 \div 1 =$ ___
t. $8 * 4 =$ ___	t. $40 \div 4 =$ ___	t. $1 * 9 =$ ___	t. $0 / 0 =$ ___

Dashes 5–8

▶ **PATH to FLUENCY** **Dashes 9–12**

Complete each Dash. Check your answers on page 82.

Dash 9 2s, 5s, 9s, 10s Multiplications	Dash 10 2s, 5s, 9s, 10s Divisions	Dash 11 3s, 4s, 0s, 1s Multiplications	Dash 12 3s, 4s, 1s Divisions
a. 4 × 5 = ____	a. 8 / 2 = ____	a. 3 × 0 = ____	a. 12 / 4 = ____
b. 10 • 3 = ____	b. 50 ÷ 10 = ____	b. 4 • 6 = ____	b. 5 ÷ 1 = ____
c. 8 * 9 = ____	c. 15 / 5 = ____	c. 9 * 1 = ____	c. 21 / 3 = ____
d. 6 × 2 = ____	d. 63 ÷ 9 = ____	d. 3 × 3 = ____	d. 1 ÷ 1 = ____
e. 5 • 7 = ____	e. 90 / 10 = ____	e. 8 • 4 = ____	e. 16 / 4 = ____
f. 10 * 5 = ____	f. 90 ÷ 9 = ____	f. 0 * 5 = ____	f. 9 ÷ 3 = ____
g. 8 × 2 = ____	g. 35 / 5 = ____	g. 1 × 6 = ____	g. 32 / 4 = ____
h. 6 • 10 = ____	h. 14 ÷ 2 = ____	h. 4 • 3 = ____	h. 8 ÷ 1 = ____
i. 9 * 3 = ____	i. 27 / 9 = ____	i. 7 * 4 = ____	i. 24 / 4 = ____
j. 2 × 9 = ____	j. 45 / 5 = ____	j. 3 × 7 = ____	j. 18 / 3 = ____
k. 5 • 8 = ____	k. 10 ÷ 10 = ____	k. 0 • 1 = ____	k. 10 ÷ 1 = ____
l. 10 * 7 = ____	l. 25 / 5 = ____	l. 10 * 1 = ____	l. 40 / 4 = ____
m. 5 × 5 = ____	m. 54 ÷ 9 = ____	m. 4 × 4 = ____	m. 12 ÷ 3 = ____
n. 1 • 5 = ____	n. 6 / 2 = ____	n. 9 • 3 = ____	n. 6 / 3 = ____
o. 9 * 6 = ____	o. 72 ÷ 9 = ____	o. 8 * 0 = ____	o. 4 ÷ 4 = ____
p. 10 × 10 = ____	p. 40 / 5 = ____	p. 5 × 4 = ____	p. 7 / 1 = ____
q. 4 • 2 = ____	q. 80 ÷ 10 = ____	q. 1 • 6 = ____	q. 28 ÷ 4 = ____
r. 10 * 8 = ____	r. 18 ÷ 2 = ____	r. 3 * 8 = ____	r. 24 ÷ 3 = ____
s. 3 × 9 = ____	s. 36 / 9 = ____	s. 4 × 9 = ____	s. 20 / 4 = ____
t. 9 • 9 = ____	t. 30 ÷ 5 = ____	t. 0 • 4 = ____	t. 27 ÷ 3 = ____

Name _____   Date _____

► ⟨PATH to FLUENCY⟩ **Dashes 9A–12A**

Complete each Dash. Check your answers on page 82.

Dash 9A **2s, 5s, 9s, 10s** **Multiplications**	**Dash 10A** **2s, 5s, 9s, 10s** **Divisions**	**Dash 11A** **3s, 4s, 0s, 1s** **Multiplications**	**Dash 12A** **3s, 4s, 1s** **Divisions**
a. 9 × 9 = _____	a. 30 / 5 = _____	a. 0 × 4 = _____	a. 10 / 1 = _____
b. 4 * 5 = _____	b. 18 ÷ 2 = _____	b. 4 * 9 = _____	b. 40 ÷ 4 = _____
c. 10 • 3 = _____	c. 40 / 5 = _____	c. 3 • 8 = _____	c. 12 / 3 = _____
d. 3 × 9 = _____	d. 6 ÷ 2 = _____	d. 3 × 0 = _____	d. 6 ÷ 3 = _____
e. 10 * 8 = _____	e. 25 / 5 = _____	e. 4 * 6 = _____	e. 4 / 4 = _____
f. 6 • 2 = _____	f. 45 ÷ 5 = _____	f. 9 • 1 = _____	f. 7 ÷ 1 = _____
g. 8 × 9 = _____	g. 14 / 2 = _____	g. 3 × 3 = _____	g. 28 / 4 = _____
h. 4 * 2 = _____	h. 90 ÷ 9 = _____	h. 8 * 4 = _____	h. 24 ÷ 3 = _____
i. 10 • 10 = _____	i. 63 / 9 = _____	i. 0 • 5 = _____	i. 20 / 4 = _____
j. 9 × 6 = _____	j. 50 ÷ 10 = _____	j. 1 × 6 = _____	j. 27 ÷ 3 = _____
k. 5 * 7 = _____	k. 8 / 2 = _____	k. 5 * 4 = _____	k. 12 / 4 = _____
l. 10 • 5 = _____	l. 15 ÷ 5 = _____	l. 8 • 0 = _____	l. 5 ÷ 1 = _____
m. 8 × 2 = _____	m. 90 / 10 = _____	m. 9 × 3 = _____	m. 21 / 3 = _____
n. 6 * 10 = _____	n. 35 ÷ 5 = _____	n. 4 * 4 = _____	n. 1 ÷ 1 = _____
o. 2 * 9 = _____	o. 27 / 9 = _____	o. 10 • 1 = _____	o. 16 / 4 = _____
p. 9 • 6 = _____	p. 10 ÷ 10 = _____	p. 4 × 3 = _____	p. 9 ÷ 3 = _____
q. 1 × 5 = _____	q. 54 / 9 = _____	q. 7 * 4 = _____	q. 32 / 4 = _____
r. 5 * 5 = _____	r. 72 ÷ 9 = _____	r. 3 • 7 = _____	r. 8 ÷ 1 = _____
s. 10 • 7 = _____	s. 80 / 10 = _____	s. 0 × 1 = _____	s. 24 / 4 = _____
t. 5 × 8 = _____	t. 36 ÷ 9 = _____	t. 10 * 1 = _____	t. 18 ÷ 3 = _____

Dashes 9A–12A

► Answers to Dashes 1–8

Use this sheet to check your answers to the Dashes on pages 77 and 78.

Dash 1 2s and 5s ×	Dash 2 2s and 5s ÷	Dash 3 9s and 10s ×	Dash 4 9s and 10s ÷	Dash 5 3s and 4s ×	Dash 6 3s and 4s ÷	Dash 7 0s and 1s ×	Dash 8 1s and $n \div n$ ÷
a. 12	a. 9	a. 90	a. 10	a. 27	a. 3	a. 0	a. 1
b. 45	b. 5	b. 30	b. 1	b. 8	b. 5	b. 4	b. 8
c. 14	c. 4	c. 9	c. 3	c. 18	c. 7	c. 0	c. 1
d. 40	d. 9	d. 20	d. 9	d. 40	d. 4	d. 8	d. 6
e. 8	e. 8	e. 81	e. 7	e. 3	e. 3	e. 0	e. 1
f. 15	f. 4	f. 60	f. 5	f. 4	f. 8	f. 3	f. 4
g. 2	g. 2	g. 36	g. 1	g. 30	g. 6	g. 0	g. 1
h. 35	h. 8	h. 100	h. 6	h. 20	h. 6	h. 2	h. 2
i. 18	i. 10	i. 18	i. 5	i. 9	i. 10	i. 0	i. 1
j. 20	j. 7	j. 10	j. 3	j. 16	j. 4	j. 10	j. 9
k. 10	k. 3	k. 63	k. 2	k. 24	k. 2	k. 0	k. 1
l. 5	l. 3	l. 50	l. 8	l. 28	l. 7	l. 1	l. 5
m. 4	m. 7	m. 72	m. 4	m. 6	m. 8	m. 0	m. 1
n. 50	n. 1	n. 70	n. 2	n. 36	n. 5	n. 5	n. 1
o. 20	o. 5	o. 27	o. 6	o. 21	o. 9	o. 0	o. 7
p. 30	p. 2	p. 40	p. 10	p. 12	p. 5	p. 6	p. 1
q. 6	q. 3	q. 45	q. 9	q. 15	q. 9	q. 0	q. 10
r. 25	r. 6	r. 80	r. 7	r. 24	r. 9	r. 0	r. 1
s. 16	s. 1	s. 54	s. 8	s. 12	s. 2	s. 7	s. 3
t. 30	t. 9	t. 90	t. 4	t. 32	t. 10	t. 9	t. 0

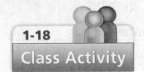
▶ Answers to Dashes 9–12, 9A–12A

Use this sheet to check your answers to the Dashes on pages 79 and 80.

Dash 9 ×	Dash 10 ÷	Dash 11 ×	Dash 12 ÷	Dash 9A ×	Dash 10A ÷	Dash 11A ×	Dash 12A ÷
a. 20	a. 4	a. 0	a. 3	a. 81	a. 6	a. 0	a. 10
b. 30	b. 5	b. 24	b. 5	b. 20	b. 9	b. 36	b. 10
c. 72	c. 3	c. 9	c. 7	c. 30	c. 8	c. 24	c. 4
d. 12	d. 7	d. 9	d. 1	d. 27	d. 3	d. 0	d. 2
e. 35	e. 9	e. 32	e. 4	e. 80	e. 5	e. 24	e. 1
f. 50	f. 10	f. 0	f. 3	f. 12	f. 9	f. 9	f. 7
g. 16	g. 7	g. 6	g. 8	g. 72	g. 7	g. 9	g. 7
h. 60	h. 7	h. 12	h. 8	h. 8	h. 10	h. 32	h. 8
i. 27	i. 3	i. 28	i. 6	i. 100	i. 7	i. 0	i. 5
j. 18	j. 9	j. 21	j. 6	j. 54	j. 5	j. 6	j. 9
k. 40	k. 1	k. 0	k. 10	k. 35	k. 4	k. 20	k. 3
l. 70	l. 5	l. 10	l. 10	l. 50	l. 3	l. 0	l. 5
m. 25	m. 6	m. 16	m. 4	m. 16	m. 9	m. 27	m. 7
n. 5	n. 3	n. 27	n. 2	n. 60	n. 7	n. 16	n. 1
o. 54	o. 8	o. 0	o. 1	o. 18	o. 3	o. 10	o. 4
p. 100	p. 8	p. 20	p. 7	p. 54	p. 1	p. 12	p. 3
q. 8	q. 8	q. 6	q. 7	q. 5	q. 6	q. 28	q. 8
r. 80	r. 9	r. 24	r. 8	r. 25	r. 8	r. 21	r. 8
s. 27	s. 4	s. 36	s. 5	s. 70	s. 8	s. 0	s. 6
t. 81	t. 6	t. 0	t. 9	t. 40	t. 4	t. 10	t. 6

Answers to Dashes 9–12, 9A–12A

▶ PATH to FLUENCY **What is Your Hobby?**

Carina asked some third graders, "What is your hobby?"
The answers are shown under the photos.

Photography
Eight more than dancing
said photography.

Games
Eight third graders said
games.

Dancing
Four third graders
said dancing.

Reading
Six less than photography said
reading.

3. Use the information above to complete the chart below.

What is Your Hobby?

Hobby	Number of Students
Dancing	
Photography	
Games	
Reading	

4. Use the chart to complete the pictograph below.

Hobbies	
Dancing	
Photography	
Games	
Reading	

Each ☐ stands for 2 third graders.

5. How many third graders answered Carina's question?

_____

▶ **Vocabulary**

Choose the best word from the box.

1. Groups that have the same number of objects in each group are called _____. (Lesson 1-2)

2. When you multiply two numbers, the answer is the _____. (Lesson 1-1)

3. The 3 and 4 in $3 \times 4 = 12$ are called _____. (Lesson 1-1)

▶ **Concepts and Skills**

4. Explain three ways to find the area of the rectangle at the right. Use the ways to find the area. (Lesson 1-11)

   _____

   _____

   _____

   _____

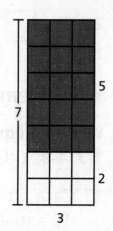

5. What pattern can you use to multiply a number and 9 if you know 10 times the number? Give an example. (Lesson 1-8)

   _____

   _____

Write and solve a multiplication equation with an unknown to find the answer. (Lessons 1-4, 1-5, 1-6, 1-7)

6. $18 \div \boxed{} = 9$

7. $54 \div 9 = \boxed{}$

Multiply or divide.

(Lessons 1-1, 1-4, 1-5, 1-6, 1-7, 1-9, 1-10, 1-12, 1-14, 1-15, 1-18)

8. $8 \times 2 =$ ☐

9. $5 \cdot 7 =$ ☐

10. $10 \div 1 =$ ☐

11. $81 \div 9 =$ ☐

12. $4 \times 0 =$ ☐

13. $63/9 =$ ☐

14. $6 \cdot 4 =$ ☐

15. $45/5 =$ ☐

16. ☐ $3\overline{)24}$

17. ☐ $\times 3 = 27$

18. $28 \div$ ☐ $= 7$

19. $10 \cdot$ ☐ $= 80$

20. $6 \times$ ☐ $= 18$

21. $35/5 =$ ☐

22. ☐ $\times 6 = 30$

▶ Problem Solving

Write an equation and solve the problem. (Lessons 1-4, 1-5, 1-6, 1-7, 1-8, 1-9, 1-10, 1-12, 1-14, 1-15, 1-16, 1-18)

23. Zara arranged 80 stamps of her stamp collection in 10 equal rows. How many stamps were in each row?

_____

24. Olivia's CD rack has 4 shelves. It holds 8 CDs on a shelf. How many CDs will fit in the rack altogether?

_____

25. **Extended Response** Paco set up 7 tables to seat 28 children at his birthday party. The same number of children will sit at each table. How many children will sit at each table? Explain how you found your answer. Make a math drawing to help.

_____

_____

Family Letter

Dear Family,

In this unit, students learn multiplications and divisions for 6s, 7s, and 8s, while continuing to practice the rest of the basic multiplications and divisions covered in Unit 1.

Although students practice all the 6s, 7s, and 8s multiplications, they really have only six new multiplications to learn: 6×6, 6×7, 6×8, 7×7, 7×8, and 8×8. The lessons for these multiplications focus on strategies for finding the products using multiplications they know.

This unit also focuses on word problems. Students are presented with a variety of one-step and two-step word problems.

Here is an example of a two-step problem:

A roller coaster has 7 cars. Each car has 4 seats. If there were 3 empty seats, how many people were on the roller coaster?

Students use the language and context of each problem to determine which operation or operations—multiplication, division, addition, or subtraction—they must use to solve it. Students use a variety of methods to solve two-step word problems.

Please continue to help your child get faster on multiplications and divisions. Use all of the practice materials that your child has brought home. Your support is crucial to your child's learning.

Please call if you have any questions or comments.

Thank you.

Sincerely,
Your child's teacher

© Houghton Mifflin Harcourt Publishing Company

COMMON CORE

This unit includes the Common Core Standards for Mathematical Content for Operations and Algebraic Thinking, 3.OA.1, 3.OA.2, 3.OA.3, 3.OA.4, 3.OA.5, 3.OA.6, 3.OA.7, 3.OA.8, 3.OA.9; Number and Operations in Base Ten, 3.NBT.3; Measurement and Data, 3.MD.5a, 3.MD.5b, 3.MD.7a, 3.MD.7b and all Mathematical Practices

Carta a la familia

Estimada familia:

En esta unidad los estudiantes aprenden las multiplicaciones y divisiones con el 6, el 7 y el 8, mientras siguen practicando las demás multiplicaciones y divisiones que se presentaron en la Unidad 1.

Aunque los estudiantes practican todas las multiplicaciones con el 6, el 7 y el 8, en realidad sólo tienen que aprender seis multiplicaciones nuevas: 6×6, 6×7, 6×8, 7×7, 7×8 y 8×8. Las lecciones acerca de estas multiplicaciones se centran en estrategias para hallar los productos usando multiplicaciones que ya se conocen.

Esta unidad también se centra en problemas verbales. A los estudiantes se les presenta una variedad de problemas de uno y de dos pasos.

Este es un ejemplo de un problema de dos pasos:
Una montaña rusa tiene 7 carros. Cada carro tiene 7 asientos. Si hay 3 asientos vacíos. Cuántas personas había en la montaña rusa?

Los estudiantes aprovechan el lenguaje y el contexto de cada problema para determinar qué operación u operaciones deben usar para resolverlo: multiplicación, división, suma o resta. Los estudiantes usan una variedad de métodos para resolver problemas de dos pasos.

Por favor continúe ayudando a su niño a practicar las multiplicaciones y las divisiones. Use todos los materiales de práctica que su niño ha llevado a casa. Su apoyo es importante para el aprendizaje de su niño.

Si tiene alguna duda o pregunta, por favor comuníquese conmigo.

Atentamente,
El maestro de su niño

© Houghton Mifflin Harcourt Publishing Company

COMMON CORE

Esta unidad incluye los Common Core Standards for Mathematical Content for Operations and Algebraic Thinking, 3.OA.1, 3.OA.2, 3.OA.3, 3.OA.4, 3.OA.5, 3.OA.6, 3.OA.7, 3.OA.8, 3.OA.9; Number and Operations in Base Ten, 3.NBT.3; Measurement and Data, 3.MD.5a, 3.MD.5b, 3.MD.7a, 3.MD.7b and all Mathematical Practices

70 UNIT 2 LESSON 1   Multiply and Divide with 6

Study Sheet C

7s

Count-bys	Mixed Up ×	Mixed Up ÷
$1 \times 7 = 7$	$6 \times 7 = 42$	$70 \div 7 = 10$
$2 \times 7 = 14$	$8 \times 7 = 56$	$14 \div 7 = 2$
$3 \times 7 = 21$	$5 \times 7 = 35$	$28 \div 7 = 4$
$4 \times 7 = 28$	$9 \times 7 = 63$	$56 \div 7 = 8$
$5 \times 7 = 35$	$4 \times 7 = 28$	$42 \div 7 = 6$
$6 \times 7 = 42$	$10 \times 7 = 70$	$63 \div 7 = 9$
$7 \times 7 = 49$	$3 \times 7 = 21$	$21 \div 7 = 3$
$8 \times 7 = 56$	$1 \times 7 = 7$	$49 \div 7 = 7$
$9 \times 7 = 63$	$7 \times 7 = 49$	$7 \div 7 = 1$
$10 \times 7 = 70$	$2 \times 7 = 14$	$35 \div 7 = 5$

Squares

Count-bys	Mixed Up ×	Mixed Up ÷
$1 \times 1 = 1$	$3 \times 3 = 9$	$25 \div 5 = 5$
$2 \times 2 = 4$	$9 \times 9 = 81$	$4 \div 2 = 2$
$3 \times 3 = 9$	$4 \times 4 = 16$	$81 \div 9 = 9$
$4 \times 4 = 16$	$6 \times 6 = 36$	$9 \div 3 = 3$
$5 \times 5 = 25$	$2 \times 2 = 4$	$36 \div 6 = 6$
$6 \times 6 = 36$	$7 \times 7 = 49$	$100 \div 10 = 10$
$7 \times 7 = 49$	$10 \times 10 = 100$	$16 \div 4 = 4$
$8 \times 8 = 64$	$1 \times 1 = 1$	$49 \div 7 = 7$
$9 \times 9 = 81$	$5 \times 5 = 25$	$1 \div 1 = 1$
$10 \times 10 = 100$	$8 \times 8 = 64$	$64 \div 8 = 8$

6s

Count-bys	Mixed Up ×	Mixed Up ÷
$1 \times 6 = 6$	$10 \times 6 = 60$	$54 \div 6 = 9$
$2 \times 6 = 12$	$8 \times 6 = 48$	$30 \div 6 = 5$
$3 \times 6 = 18$	$2 \times 6 = 12$	$12 \div 6 = 2$
$4 \times 6 = 24$	$6 \times 6 = 36$	$60 \div 6 = 10$
$5 \times 6 = 30$	$4 \times 6 = 24$	$48 \div 6 = 8$
$6 \times 6 = 36$	$1 \times 6 = 6$	$36 \div 6 = 6$
$7 \times 6 = 42$	$9 \times 6 = 54$	$6 \div 6 = 1$
$8 \times 6 = 48$	$3 \times 6 = 18$	$42 \div 6 = 7$
$9 \times 6 = 54$	$7 \times 6 = 42$	$18 \div 6 = 3$
$10 \times 6 = 60$	$5 \times 6 = 30$	$24 \div 6 = 4$

8s

Count-bys	Mixed Up ×	Mixed Up ÷
$1 \times 8 = 8$	$6 \times 8 = 48$	$16 \div 8 = 2$
$2 \times 8 = 16$	$10 \times 8 = 80$	$40 \div 8 = 5$
$3 \times 8 = 24$	$7 \times 8 = 56$	$72 \div 8 = 9$
$4 \times 8 = 32$	$2 \times 8 = 16$	$32 \div 8 = 4$
$5 \times 8 = 40$	$4 \times 8 = 32$	$8 \div 8 = 1$
$6 \times 8 = 48$	$8 \times 8 = 64$	$80 \div 8 = 10$
$7 \times 8 = 56$	$5 \times 8 = 40$	$64 \div 8 = 8$
$8 \times 8 = 64$	$9 \times 8 = 72$	$24 \div 8 = 3$
$9 \times 8 = 72$	$3 \times 8 = 24$	$56 \div 8 = 7$
$10 \times 8 = 80$	$1 \times 8 = 8$	$48 \div 8 = 6$

► **PATH to FLUENCY Unknown Number Puzzles**

Complete each Unknown Number puzzle.

1.

×	5	2	
	30		48
4		8	32
	45		72

2.

×		3	
6	30		42
4			28
	40	24	56

3.

×	4		8
9		81	
	12		24
	20	45	40

4.

×		3	
	60		20
6	36		
	18	9	6

5.

×	8		2
7		28	
	16	8	
	32	16	8

6.

×	9		
8		56	24
	54	42	18
5			15

7.

×	8		7
8		40	
	32	20	28
	24	15	

8.

×	3	4	
	27	36	81
7			63
			18

9.

×			10
8	48	16	
7	42	14	
	36		60

Solve Area Word Problems

► PATH to FLUENCY **Check Sheet 7: 6s and 8s**

6s Multiplications	6s Divisions	8s Multiplications	8s Divisions
$10 \times 6 = 60$	$24 / 6 = 4$	$2 \times 8 = 16$	$72 / 8 = 9$
$6 \cdot 4 = 24$	$48 \div 6 = 8$	$8 \cdot 10 = 80$	$16 \div 8 = 2$
$6 * 7 = 42$	$60 / 6 = 10$	$3 * 8 = 24$	$40 / 8 = 5$
$2 \times 6 = 12$	$12 \div 6 = 2$	$9 \times 8 = 72$	$8 \div 8 = 1$
$6 \cdot 5 = 30$	$42 / 6 = 7$	$8 \cdot 4 = 32$	$80 / 8 = 10$
$6 * 8 = 48$	$30 \div 6 = 5$	$8 * 7 = 56$	$48 \div 8 = 6$
$9 \times 6 = 54$	$6 / 6 = 1$	$5 \times 8 = 40$	$56 / 8 = 7$
$6 \cdot 1 = 6$	$18 \div 6 = 3$	$8 \cdot 6 = 48$	$24 \div 8 = 3$
$6 * 6 = 36$	$54 / 6 = 9$	$1 * 8 = 8$	$64 / 8 = 8$
$6 \times 3 = 18$	$36 / 6 = 6$	$8 \times 8 = 64$	$32 / 8 = 4$
$6 \cdot 6 = 36$	$48 \div 6 = 8$	$4 \cdot 8 = 32$	$80 \div 8 = 10$
$5 * 6 = 30$	$12 / 6 = 2$	$6 * 8 = 48$	$56 / 8 = 7$
$6 \times 2 = 12$	$24 \div 6 = 4$	$8 \times 3 = 24$	$8 \div 8 = 1$
$4 \cdot 6 = 24$	$60 / 6 = 10$	$7 \cdot 8 = 56$	$24 / 8 = 3$
$6 * 9 = 54$	$6 \div 6 = 1$	$8 * 2 = 16$	$64 \div 8 = 8$
$8 \times 6 = 48$	$42 / 6 = 7$	$8 \times 9 = 72$	$16 / 8 = 2$
$7 \cdot 6 = 42$	$18 \div 6 = 3$	$8 \cdot 1 = 8$	$72 \div 8 = 9$
$6 * 10 = 60$	$36 \div 6 = 6$	$8 * 8 = 64$	$32 \div 8 = 4$
$1 \times 6 = 6$	$30 / 6 = 5$	$10 \times 8 = 80$	$40 / 8 = 5$
$4 \cdot 6 = 24$	$54 \div 6 = 9$	$5 \cdot 8 = 40$	$48 \div 8 = 6$

► Identify the Type and Choose the Operation

Solve. Then circle what type it is and what operation you use.

1. Students in Mr. Till's class hung their paintings on the wall. They made 6 rows, with 5 paintings in each row. How many paintings did the students hang?

   _____

   Circle one: array   equal groups   area
   Circle one: multiplication   division

2. Write your own problem that is the same type as problem 1. _____

   _____

   _____

3. There are 8 goldfish in each tank at the pet store. If there are 56 goldfish in all, how many tanks are there?

   _____

   Circle one: array   equal groups   area
   Circle one: multiplication   division

4. Write your own problem that is the same type as problem 3. _____

   _____

   _____

5. Pierre built a rectangular pen for his rabbits. The pen is 4 feet wide and 6 feet long. What is the area of the pen? _____

   Circle one: array   equal groups   area
   Circle one: multiplication   division

Name ______________________ Date ______________

PATH to FLUENCY

► Identify the Type and Choose the Operation (continued)

6. Write your own problem that is the same type as problem 5. ______________________

____

____

____

7. Paulo arranged 72 baseball cards in 9 rows and a certain number of columns. Into how many columns did he arrange the cards? ______________

Circle one: array equal groups area
Circle one: multiplication division

8. Write your own problem that is the same type as Problem 7. ______________________

____

____

____

9. The store sells bottles of juice in six-packs. Mr. Lee bought 9 six-packs for a picnic. How many bottles did he buy? ______________

Circle one: array equal groups area
Circle one: multiplication division

10. Write your own problem that is the same type as Problem 9. ______________________

____

____

____

11. **Math Journal** Write an area multiplication problem. Draw a Fast Array to solve it.

► PATH to FLUENCY **Check Sheet 8: 7s and Squares**

7s Multiplications	7s Divisions	Squares Multiplications	Squares Divisions
$4 \times 7 = 28$	$14 / 7 = 2$	$8 \times 8 = 64$	$81 / 9 = 9$
$7 \cdot 2 = 14$	$28 \div 7 = 4$	$10 \cdot 10 = 100$	$4 \div 2 = 2$
$7 * 8 = 56$	$70 / 7 = 10$	$3 * 3 = 9$	$25 / 5 = 5$
$7 \times 7 = 49$	$56 \div 7 = 8$	$9 \times 9 = 81$	$1 \div 1 = 1$
$7 \cdot 1 = 7$	$42 / 7 = 6$	$4 \cdot 4 = 16$	$100 / 10 = 10$
$7 * 10 = 70$	$63 \div 7 = 9$	$7 * 7 = 49$	$36 \div 6 = 6$
$3 \times 7 = 21$	$7 / 7 = 1$	$5 \times 5 = 25$	$49 / 7 = 7$
$7 \cdot 6 = 42$	$49 \div 7 = 7$	$6 \cdot 6 = 36$	$9 \div 3 = 3$
$5 * 7 = 35$	$21 / 7 = 3$	$1 * 1 = 1$	$64 / 8 = 8$
$7 \times 9 = 63$	$35 / 7 = 5$	$5 * 5 = 25$	$16 / 4 = 4$
$7 \cdot 4 = 28$	$7 \div 7 = 1$	$1 \cdot 1 = 1$	$100 \div 10 = 10$
$9 * 7 = 63$	$63 / 7 = 9$	$3 \cdot 3 = 9$	$49 / 7 = 7$
$2 \times 7 = 14$	$14 \div 7 = 2$	$10 \times 10 = 100$	$1 \div 1 = 1$
$7 \cdot 5 = 35$	$70 / 7 = 10$	$4 \times 4 = 16$	$9 / 3 = 3$
$8 * 7 = 56$	$21 \div 7 = 3$	$9 * 9 = 81$	$64 \div 8 = 8$
$7 \times 3 = 21$	$49 / 7 = 7$	$2 \times 2 = 4$	$4 / 2 = 2$
$6 \cdot 7 = 42$	$28 \div 7 = 4$	$6 * 6 = 36$	$81 \div 9 = 9$
$10 * 7 = 70$	$56 \div 7 = 8$	$7 \times 7 = 49$	$16 \div 4 = 4$
$1 \times 7 = 7$	$35 / 7 = 5$	$5 \cdot 5 = 25$	$25 / 5 = 5$
$7 \cdot 7 = 49$	$42 \div 7 = 6$	$8 \cdot 8 = 64$	$36 \div 6 = 6$

VOCABULARY
square numbers

▶ Look for Patterns

11. List the products in Exercises 1–10 in order.
Discuss the patterns you see with your class.

_____

The numbers you listed in Exercise 11 are called
square numbers because they are the areas of
squares with whole-number lengths of sides.
A square number is the product of a whole
number and itself. So, if n is a whole number,
$n \times n$ is a square number.

▶ Patterns on the Multiplication Table

12. In the table below, circle the products that are
square numbers. Discuss the patterns you see
with your class.

X	1	2	3	4	5	6	7	8	9	10
1	1	2	3	4	5	6	7	8	9	10
2	2	4	6	8	10	12	14	16	18	20
3	3	6	9	12	15	18	21	24	27	30
4	4	8	12	16	20	24	28	32	36	40
5	5	10	15	20	25	30	35	40	45	50
6	6	12	18	24	30	36	42	48	54	60
7	7	14	21	28	35	42	49	56	63	70
8	8	16	24	32	40	48	56	64	72	80
9	9	18	27	36	45	54	63	72	81	90
10	10	20	30	40	50	60	70	80	90	100

Name _____ **Date** _____

► PATH to FLUENCY **Check Sheet 9: 6s, 7s, and 8s**

6s, 7s, and 8s Multiplications	6s, 7s, and 8s Multiplications	6s, 7s, and 8s Divisions	6s, 7s, and 8s Divisions
1 × 6 = 6	0 × 8 = 0	24 / 6 = 4	54 / 6 = 9
6 • 7 = 42	6 • 2 = 12	21 ÷ 7 = 3	24 ÷ 8 = 3
3 * 8 = 24	4 * 7 = 28	16 / 8 = 2	14 / 7 = 2
6 × 2 = 12	8 × 3 = 24	24 ÷ 8 = 3	32 ÷ 8 = 4
7 • 5 = 35	5 • 6 = 30	14 / 7 = 2	18 / 6 = 3
8 * 4 = 32	7 * 2 = 14	30 ÷ 6 = 5	56 ÷ 7 = 8
6 × 6 = 36	3 × 8 = 24	35 / 7 = 5	40 / 8 = 5
8 • 7 = 56	6 • 4 = 24	24 ÷ 8 = 3	35 ÷ 7 = 5
9 * 8 = 72	0 * 7 = 0	18 / 6 = 3	12 / 6 = 2
6 × 10 = 60	8 × 1 = 8	12 / 6 = 2	21 / 7 = 3
7 • 1 = 7	8 • 6 = 48	42 ÷ 7 = 6	16 ÷ 8 = 2
8 * 3 = 24	7 * 9 = 63	56 / 8 = 7	42 / 6 = 7
5 × 6 = 30	10 × 8 = 80	49 ÷ 7 = 7	80 ÷ 8 = 10
4 • 7 = 28	6 • 10 = 60	16 / 8 = 2	36 / 6 = 6
2 * 8 = 16	3 * 7 = 21	60 ÷ 6 = 10	7 ÷ 7 = 1
7 × 7 = 49	8 × 4 = 32	54 / 6 = 9	64 / 8 = 8
7 • 6 = 42	6 • 5 = 30	8 ÷ 8 = 1	24 ÷ 6 = 4
8 * 8 = 64	7 * 4 = 28	28 ÷ 7 = 4	21 ÷ 7 = 3
9 × 6 = 54	8 × 8 = 64	72 / 8 = 9	49 / 7 = 7
10 • 7 = 70	6 • 9 = 54	56 ÷ 7 = 8	24 ÷ 8 = 3

► PATH to FLUENCY **Check Sheet 10: 0s–10s**

0s–10s Multiplications	0s–10s Multiplications	0s–10s Divisions	0s–10s Divisions
9 × 0 = 0	9 × 4 = 36	9 / 1 = 9	90 / 10 = 9
1 • 1 = 1	5 • 9 = 45	12 ÷ 3 = 4	64 ÷ 8 = 8
2 * 3 = 6	6 * 10 = 60	14 / 2 = 7	15 / 5 = 3
1 × 3 = 3	7 × 3 = 21	20 ÷ 4 = 5	12 ÷ 6 = 2
5 • 4 = 20	5 • 3 = 15	10 / 5 = 2	14 / 7 = 2
7 * 5 = 35	4 * 1 = 4	48 ÷ 8 = 6	45 ÷ 9 = 5
6 × 9 = 54	7 × 5 = 35	35 / 7 = 5	8 / 1 = 8
4 • 7 = 28	6 • 3 = 18	60 ÷ 6 = 10	30 ÷ 3 = 10
1 * 8 = 8	8 * 7 = 56	81 / 9 = 9	16 / 4 = 4
9 × 8 = 72	5 × 8 = 40	20 / 10 = 2	8 / 2 = 4
2 • 10 = 20	9 • 9 = 81	16 ÷ 2 = 8	80 ÷ 10 = 8
0 * 7 = 0	9 * 10 = 90	30 / 5 = 6	36 / 4 = 9
4 × 1 = 4	0 × 0 = 0	49 ÷ 7 = 7	25 ÷ 5 = 5
2 • 4 = 8	1 • 0 = 0	60 / 6 = 10	42 / 7 = 6
10 * 3 = 30	1 * 6 = 6	30 ÷ 3 = 10	36 ÷ 6 = 6
8 × 4 = 32	7 × 2 = 14	8 / 1 = 8	90 / 9 = 10
5 • 8 = 40	6 • 3 = 18	16 ÷ 4 = 4	24 ÷ 8 = 3
4 * 6 = 24	4 * 5 = 20	16 ÷ 8 = 2	6 ÷ 2 = 3
7 × 6 = 42	6 × 6 = 36	40 / 10 = 4	9 / 3 = 3
1 • 8 = 8	10 • 7 = 70	36 ÷ 9 = 4	1 ÷ 1 = 1

► PATH to FLUENCY **Play Quotient Match and Division Blockout**

Read the rules for playing a game.
Then play the game with your partner.

Rules for Quotient Match

Number of players: 2 or 3

What each player will need: Division Strategy Cards for 6s, 7s, and 8s

1. Shuffle the cards. Put the division cards, without answers side up, on the table in 6 rows of 4.

2. Players take turns. On each turn, a player chooses three cards that he or she thinks have the same quotient and turns them over.

3. If all three cards do have the same quotient the player takes them. If the cards do not have the same quotient, the player turns them back over so the without answers side is up.

4. Play continues until no cards remain.

Rules for Division Blockout

Number of players: 3

What each player will need: Blockout Game Board (TRB M70), Division Strategy Cards for 6s, 7s, and 8s

1. Players do not write anything on the game board. The first row is for 6s, the second row for 7s, and the third row for 8s, as indicated in the gray column on the left.

2. Each player shuffles his or her Division Strategy Cards for 6s, 7s, 8s, making sure the division sides without answers are up.

3. Repeat Steps 2, 3, and 4 above. This time players will place the Strategy Cards in the appropriate row to indicate whether the unknown factor is 6, 7, or 8.

▶ **PATH to FLUENCY** Play Multiplication Blockout

Read the rules for playing *Multiplication Blockout*. Then play the game with your partner.

Rules for *Multiplication Block Out*

Number of players: 3

What each player will need: *Blockout* Game Board (TRB M70), Multiplication Strategy Cards for 6s, 7s, and 8s

1. Players choose any 5 factors from 2–9 and write them in any order in the gray spaces at the top of the game board. The players then write the products in the large white spaces. The result will be a scrambled multiplication table.

2. Once the table is complete, players cut off the gray row and gray column that show the factors so that only the products are showing. This will be the game board.

3. Each player shuffles his or her Multiplication Strategy Cards for 6s, 7s, and 8s, making sure the multiplication sides without answers are facing up.

4. One player says, "Go!" and everyone quickly places their Strategy Cards on the game board spaces showing the corresponding products. When a player's game board is completely filled, he or she shouts, "Blockout!"

5. Everyone stops and checks the player's work. If all the cards are placed correctly, that player is the winner. If the player has made a mistake, he or she sits out and waits for the next player to shout, "Blockout!"

2-8
Class Activity

Name Date

► PATH to FLUENCY Complete a Multiplication Table

1. Look at the factors to complete the Multiplication Table.
Leave blanks for the products you do not know.

×	1	2	3	4	5	6	7	8	9	10
1										
2										
3										
4										
5										
6										
7										
8										
9										
10										

2. Write the multiplications you need to practice.

Name _____ Date _____

▶ PATH to FLUENCY **Scrambled Multiplication Tables**

The factors are at the side and top of each table.
The products are in the white boxes.

Complete each table.

A

×										
	6	30	54	60	42	24	18	12	48	36
	2	10	18	20	14	8	6	4	16	12
	10	50	90	100	70	40	30	20	80	60
	8	40	72	80	56	32	24	16	64	48
	5	25	45	50	35	20	15	10	40	30
	1	5	9	10	7	4	3	2	8	6
	9	45	81	90	63	36	27	18	72	54
	4	20	36	40	28	16	12	8	32	24
	7	35	63	70	49	28	21	14	56	42
	3	15	27	30	21	12	9	6	24	18

B

×										
	27	6	24	21	18	15	12	9	3	
	36	8	32	28	24		16	12	4	40
	9	2	8	7	6	5	4	3	1	10
	18	4	16	14		10	8	6	2	20
		14	56	49	42		28	21	7	
	72		64	56	48	40	32	24	8	80
	45	10	40		30	25	20	15	5	
	54	12	48	42	36	30	24	18	6	60
	90		80	70	60		40	30	10	100
	81	18	72		54	45	36	27	9	

C

×										
	100		20		70	50		90		10
	50	15		20	35		30		40	5
	10	3		4	7		6	9		1
		9		12	21	15		27	24	
		6	4	8			12	18	16	2
		12	8	16	28	20		36	32	
	90	27	18	36	63	45	54		72	
		18	12	24		30	36	54	48	6
		21		28	49		42		56	7
		24		32	56	40		72	64	8

D

×										
	48		42	12	36		18	6		30
	56	28		14		70	21		63	35
			70		60			10		50
		20	35		30		15	5	45	
	32			8		40			36	
	8	4		2			3	1		5
		8	14		12		6		18	10
	64		56		48	80	24	8		40
	72	36		18			27		81	
	24		21		18	30		3	27	

Name

Date

► **PATH to FLUENCY Dashes 13–16**

Complete each Dash. Check your answers on page 125.

Dash 13 6s and 8s Multiplications	Dash 14 6s and 8s Divisions	Dash 15 7s and 8s Multiplications	Dash 16 7s and 8s Divisions
a. $6 \times 9 =$ _____	a. $72 / 8 =$ _____	a. $7 \times 3 =$ _____	a. $63 / 7 =$ _____
b. $8 * 2 =$ _____	b. $12 \div 6 =$ _____	b. $8 * 5 =$ _____	b. $80 \div 8 =$ _____
c. $4 \cdot 6 =$ _____	c. $16 / 8 =$ _____	c. $2 \cdot 7 =$ _____	c. $14 / 7 =$ _____
d. $7 \times 8 =$ _____	d. $24 \div 6 =$ _____	d. $1 \times 8 =$ _____	d. $16 \div 8 =$ _____
e. $6 * 1 =$ _____	e. $8 / 8 =$ _____	e. $7 * 9 =$ _____	e. $7 / 7 =$ _____
f. $8 \cdot 9 =$ _____	f. $6 \div 6 =$ _____	f. $8 \cdot 4 =$ _____	f. $48 \div 8 =$ _____
g. $3 \times 6 =$ _____	g. $40 / 8 =$ _____	g. $4 \times 7 =$ _____	g. $35 / 7 =$ _____
h. $4 * 8 =$ _____	h. $42 \div 6 =$ _____	h. $7 * 8 =$ _____	h. $32 \div 8 =$ _____
i. $6 \cdot 8 =$ _____	i. $24 / 8 =$ _____	i. $7 \cdot 1 =$ _____	i. $21 / 7 =$ _____
j. $8 \times 1 =$ _____	j. $18 \div 6 =$ _____	j. $8 \times 2 =$ _____	j. $8 \div 8 =$ _____
k. $2 * 6 =$ _____	k. $48 / 8 =$ _____	k. $5 * 7 =$ _____	k. $28 / 7 =$ _____
l. $3 \cdot 8 =$ _____	l. $48 \div 6 =$ _____	l. $9 \cdot 8 =$ _____	l. $40 \div 8 =$ _____
m. $6 \times 5 =$ _____	m. $64 / 8 =$ _____	m. $7 \times 6 =$ _____	m. $49 / 7 =$ _____
n. $8 * 8 =$ _____	n. $42 \div 6 =$ _____	n. $8 * 3 =$ _____	n. $72 \div 8 =$ _____
o. $6 \cdot 6 =$ _____	o. $56 / 8 =$ _____	o. $7 \cdot 7 =$ _____	o. $42 / 7 =$ _____
p. $5 \times 8 =$ _____	p. $30 \div 6 =$ _____	p. $8 \times 8 =$ _____	p. $24 \div 8 =$ _____
q. $6 * 7 =$ _____	q. $32 / 8 =$ _____	q. $7 * 0 =$ _____	q. $56 / 7 =$ _____
r. $8 \times 0 =$ _____	r. $54 \div 6 =$ _____	r. $6 \cdot 8 =$ _____	r. $64 \div 8 =$ _____
s. $0 * 6 =$ _____	s. $80 / 8 =$ _____	s. $8 \times 0 =$ _____	s. $70 / 7 =$ _____
t. $6 \cdot 10 =$ _____	t. $60 \div 6 =$ _____	t. $7 * 10 =$ _____	t. $56 \div 8 =$ _____

© Houghton Mifflin Harcourt Publishing Company

Name _____   Date _____

► **PATH to FLUENCY** **Dashes 17–20**

Complete each Dash. Check your answers on page 125.

Dash 17 6s and 7s Multiplications	Dash 18 6s and 7s Divisions	Dash 19 6s, 7s, 8s Multiplications	Dash 20 6s, 7s, 8s Divisions
a. $6 \times 6 =$ _____	a. $70 / 7 =$ _____	a. $7 \times 7 =$ _____	a. $21 / 7 =$ _____
b. $7 * 7 =$ _____	b. $60 \div 6 =$ _____	b. $6 \cdot 3 =$ _____	b. $16 \div 8 =$ _____
c. $3 \cdot 6 =$ _____	c. $28 / 7 =$ _____	c. $8 * 6 =$ _____	c. $54 / 6 =$ _____
d. $8 \times 7 =$ _____	d. $30 \div 6 =$ _____	d. $6 \times 6 =$ _____	d. $48 \div 8 =$ _____
e. $6 * 1 =$ _____	e. $42 / 7 =$ _____	e. $7 \cdot 6 =$ _____	e. $64 / 8 =$ _____
f. $7 \cdot 2 =$ _____	f. $24 \div 6 =$ _____	f. $4 * 7 =$ _____	f. $42 \div 6 =$ _____
g. $9 \times 6 =$ _____	g. $35 / 7 =$ _____	g. $9 \times 7 =$ _____	g. $56 / 7 =$ _____
h. $9 * 7 =$ _____	h. $12 \div 6 =$ _____	h. $6 \cdot 9 =$ _____	h. $72 \div 8 =$ _____
i. $6 \cdot 8 =$ _____	i. $7 / 7 =$ _____	i. $6 * 4 =$ _____	i. $18 / 6 =$ _____
j. $7 \times 3 =$ _____	j. $36 \div 6 =$ _____	j. $8 \times 8 =$ _____	j. $28 / 7 =$ _____
k. $7 * 6 =$ _____	k. $21 / 7 =$ _____	k. $7 \cdot 3 =$ _____	k. $56 \div 8 =$ _____
l. $1 \cdot 7 =$ _____	l. $48 \div 6 =$ _____	l. $8 * 7 =$ _____	l. $30 / 6 =$ _____
m. $6 \times 2 =$ _____	m. $63 / 7 =$ _____	m. $6 \times 7 =$ _____	m. $63 \div 7 =$ _____
n. $7 * 5 =$ _____	n. $6 \div 6 =$ _____	n. $3 \cdot 6 =$ _____	n. $32 / 8 =$ _____
o. $4 \cdot 6 =$ _____	o. $56 / 7 =$ _____	o. $2 * 7 =$ _____	o. $48 \div 6 =$ _____
p. $6 \times 7 =$ _____	p. $18 \div 6 =$ _____	p. $9 \times 8 =$ _____	p. $49 / 7 =$ _____
q. $6 * 5 =$ _____	q. $49 / 7 =$ _____	q. $5 \cdot 6 =$ _____	q. $36 \div 6 =$ _____
r. $7 \cdot 4 =$ _____	r. $42 \div 6 =$ _____	r. $7 * 8 =$ _____	r. $24 \div 8 =$ _____
s. $6 \times 10 =$ _____	s. $14 / 7 =$ _____	s. $3 \times 7 =$ _____	s. $42 / 7 =$ _____
t. $7 \times 10 =$ _____	t. $54 \div 6 =$ _____	t. $9 \cdot 6 =$ _____	t. $24 \div 6 =$ _____

► **PATH to FLUENCY** **Dashes 9B–12B**

Complete each multiplication and division Dash.
Check your answers on page 126.

Dash 9B **2s, 5s, 9s, 10s** **Multiplications**	**Dash 10B** **2s, 5s, 9s, 10s** **Divisions**	**Dash 11B** **0s, 1s, 3s, 4s** **Multiplications**	**Dash 12B** **1s, 3s, 4s** **Divisions**
a. $6 \times 2 =$ ___	a. $18 / 2 =$ ___	a. $7 \times 1 =$ ___	a. $2 / 1 =$ ___
b. $9 \cdot 4 =$ ___	b. $25 \div 5 =$ ___	b. $0 \cdot 6 =$ ___	b. $28 \div 4 =$ ___
c. $8 * 5 =$ ___	c. $70 / 10 =$ ___	c. $4 * 4 =$ ___	c. $3 / 3 =$ ___
d. $1 \times 10 =$ ___	d. $54 \div 9 =$ ___	d. $7 \times 3 =$ ___	d. $1 \div 1 =$ ___
e. $2 \cdot 7 =$ ___	e. $50 / 5 =$ ___	e. $3 \cdot 1 =$ ___	e. $40 / 4 =$ ___
f. $9 * 9 =$ ___	f. $81 \div 9 =$ ___	f. $4 * 7 =$ ___	f. $21 \div 3 =$ ___
g. $5 \times 6 =$ ___	g. $8 / 2 =$ ___	g. $9 \times 0 =$ ___	g. $5 / 1 =$ ___
h. $10 \cdot 4 =$ ___	h. $90 \div 10 =$ ___	h. $1 \cdot 1 =$ ___	h. $16 \div 4 =$ ___
i. $7 * 5 =$ ___	i. $35 / 5 =$ ___	i. $3 * 4 =$ ___	i. $15 / 3 =$ ___
j. $8 \times 2 =$ ___	j. $27 / 9 =$ ___	j. $4 \times 9 =$ ___	j. $6 / 1 =$ ___
k. $10 \cdot 10 =$ ___	k. $2 \div 2 =$ ___	k. $8 \cdot 1 =$ ___	k. $12 \div 4 =$ ___
l. $5 * 3 =$ ___	l. $36 / 9 =$ ___	l. $3 * 3 =$ ___	l. $27 / 3 =$ ___
m. $9 \times 7 =$ ___	m. $45 \div 5 =$ ___	m. $0 \times 4 =$ ___	m. $9 \div 1 =$ ___
n. $9 \cdot 2 =$ ___	n. $14 / 2 =$ ___	n. $10 \cdot 3 =$ ___	n. $8 / 4 =$ ___
o. $5 * 5 =$ ___	o. $20 \div 10 =$ ___	o. $6 * 4 =$ ___	o. $12 \div 3 =$ ___
p. $6 \times 9 =$ ___	p. $9 / 9 =$ ___	p. $1 \times 4 =$ ___	p. $3 / 1 =$ ___
q. $5 \cdot 2 =$ ___	q. $20 \div 5 =$ ___	q. $3 \cdot 6 =$ ___	q. $36 \div 4 =$ ___
r. $9 * 5 =$ ___	r. $45 \div 9 =$ ___	r. $4 * 8 =$ ___	r. $6 \div 3 =$ ___
s. $8 \times 10 =$ ___	s. $5 / 5 =$ ___	s. $7 \times 0 =$ ___	s. $4 / 1 =$ ___
t. $5 \cdot 10 =$ ___	t. $4 \div 2 =$ ___	t. $5 \cdot 3 =$ ___	t. $4 \div 4 =$ ___

Name _____   Date _____

► **PATH to FLUENCY** **Dashes 9C–12C**

Complete each Dash. Check your answers on page 126.

Dash 9C 2s, 5 ,9s, 10s Multiplications	Dash 10C 2s, 5, 9s, 10s Divisions	Dash 11C 0s, 1s ,3s, 4s Multiplications	Dash 12C 1s, 3s, 4s Divisions
a. $5 \times 8 =$ _____	a. $36 \div 9 =$ _____	a. $0 \times 7 =$ _____	a. $4 / 1 =$ _____
b. $9 * 9 =$ _____	b. $30 / 5 =$ _____	b. $1 * 4 =$ _____	b. $15 \div 3 =$ _____
c. $10 \cdot 7 =$ _____	c. $18 \div 2 =$ _____	c. $3 \cdot 6 =$ _____	c. $24 / 4 =$ _____
d. $4 \times 5 =$ _____	d. $80 / 10 =$ _____	d. $4 \times 9 =$ _____	d. $9 \div 1 =$ _____
e. $5 * 5 =$ _____	e. $40 \div 5 =$ _____	e. $8 * 0 =$ _____	e. $21 / 3 =$ _____
f. $10 \cdot 3 =$ _____	f. $72 / 9 =$ _____	f. $7 * 1 =$ _____	f. $12 \div 4 =$ _____
g. $1 \times 5 =$ _____	g. $6 \div 2 =$ _____	g. $4 \cdot 3 =$ _____	g. $5 / 1 =$ _____
h. $3 * 9 =$ _____	h. $54 / 9 =$ _____	h. $4 \times 4 =$ _____	h. $3 \div 3 =$ _____
i. $9 \cdot 6 =$ _____	i. $25 \div 5 =$ _____	i. $0 * 5 =$ _____	i. $32 / 4 =$ _____
j. $10 \times 8 =$ _____	j. $10 / 10 =$ _____	j. $1 \cdot 6 =$ _____	j. $2 \div 1 =$ _____
k. $2 * 9 =$ _____	k. $45 \div 5 =$ _____	k. $3 \times 2 =$ _____	k. $18 / 3 =$ _____
l. $6 \cdot 2 =$ _____	l. $27 / 9 =$ _____	l. $4 * 7 =$ _____	l. $36 \div 4 =$ _____
m. $6 \times 10 =$ _____	m. $14 \div 2 =$ _____	m. $1 \cdot 0 =$ _____	m. $7 / 1 =$ _____
n. $8 * 9 =$ _____	n. $35 / 5 =$ _____	n. $2 \times 1 =$ _____	n. $24 \div 3 =$ _____
o. $8 \cdot 2 =$ _____	o. $90 \div 9 =$ _____	o. $9 * 3 =$ _____	o. $4 / 4 =$ _____
p. $4 \times 2 =$ _____	p. $90 / 10 =$ _____	p. $2 \cdot 4 =$ _____	p. $6 \div 1 =$ _____
q. $10 * 5 =$ _____	q. $63 \div 9 =$ _____	q. $0 \times 3 =$ _____	q. $12 / 3 =$ _____
r. $10 \cdot 10 =$ _____	r. $15 / 5 =$ _____	r. $1 * 1 =$ _____	r. $20 \div 4 =$ _____
s. $9 \times 6 =$ _____	s. $50 \div 10 =$ _____	s. $3 \cdot 9 =$ _____	s. $8 / 1 =$ _____
t. $5 * 7 =$ _____	t. $8 / 2 =$ _____	t. $4 \times 5 =$ _____	t. $27 \div 3 =$ _____

► PATH to FLUENCY **Answers to Dashes 13–20**

Use this sheet to check your answers to the Dashes on pages 121 and 122.

Dash 13 ×	Dash 14 ÷	Dash 15 ×	Dash 16 ÷	Dash 17 ×	Dash 18 ÷	Dash 19 ×	Dash 20 ÷
a. 54	a. 9	a. 21	a. 9	a. 36	a. 10	a. 49	a. 3
b. 16	b. 2	b. 40	b. 10	b. 49	b. 10	b. 18	b. 2
c. 24	c. 2	c. 14	c. 2	c. 18	c. 4	c. 48	c. 9
d. 56	d. 4	d. 8	d. 2	d. 56	d. 5	d. 36	d. 6
e. 6	e. 1	e. 63	e. 1	e. 6	e. 6	e. 42	e. 8
f. 72	f. 1	f. 32	f. 6	f. 14	f. 4	f. 28	f. 7
g. 18	g. 5	g. 28	g. 5	g. 54	g. 5	g. 63	g. 8
h. 32	h. 7	h. 56	h. 4	h. 63	h. 2	h. 54	h. 9
i. 48	i. 3	i. 7	i. 3	i. 48	i. 1	i. 24	i. 3
j. 8	j. 3	j. 16	j. 1	j. 21	j. 6	j. 64	j. 4
k. 12	k. 6	k. 35	k. 4	k. 42	k. 3	k. 21	k. 7
l. 24	l. 8	l. 72	l. 5	l. 7	l. 8	l. 56	l. 5
m. 30	m. 8	m. 42	m. 7	m. 12	m. 9	m. 42	m. 9
n. 64	n. 7	n. 24	n. 9	n. 35	n. 1	n. 18	n. 4
o. 36	o. 7	o. 49	o. 6	o. 24	o. 8	o. 14	o. 8
p. 40	p. 5	p. 64	p. 3	p. 42	p. 3	p. 72	p. 7
q. 42	q. 4	q. 0	q. 8	q. 30	q. 7	q. 30	q. 6
r. 0	r. 9	r. 48	r. 8	r. 28	r. 7	r. 56	r. 3
s. 0	s. 10	s. 0	s. 10	s. 60	s. 2	s. 21	s. 6
t. 60	t. 10	t. 70	t. 7	t. 70	t. 9	t. 54	t. 4

► PATH to FLUENCY **Answers to Dashes 9B–12C**

Use this sheet to check your answers to the Dashes on pages 123 and 124.

Dash 9B ×	Dash 10B ÷	Dash 11B ×	Dash 12B ÷	Dash 9C ×	Dash 10C ÷	Dash 11C ×	Dash 12C ÷
a. 12	a. 9	a. 7	a. 2	a. 40	a. 4	a. 0	a. 4
b. 36	b. 5	b. 0	b. 7	b. 81	b. 6	b. 4	b. 5
c. 40	c. 7	c. 16	c. 1	c. 70	c. 9	c. 18	c. 6
d. 10	d. 6	d. 21	d. 1	d. 20	d. 8	d. 36	d. 9
e. 14	e. 10	e. 3	e. 10	e. 25	e. 8	e. 0	e. 7
f. 81	f. 9	f. 28	f. 7	f. 30	f. 8	f. 7	f. 3
g. 30	g. 4	g. 0	g. 5	g. 5	g. 3	g. 12	g. 5
h. 40	h. 9	h. 1	h. 4	h. 27	h. 6	h. 16	h. 1
i. 35	i. 7	i. 12	i. 5	i. 54	i. 5	i. 0	i. 8
j. 16	j. 3	j. 36	j. 6	j. 80	j. 1	j. 6	j. 2
k. 100	k. 1	k. 8	k. 3	k. 18	k. 9	k. 6	k. 6
l. 15	l. 4	l. 9	l. 9	l. 12	l. 3	l. 28	l. 9
m. 63	m. 9	m. 0	m. 9	m. 60	m. 7	m. 0	m. 7
n. 18	n. 7	n. 30	n. 2	n. 72	n. 7	n. 2	n. 8
o. 25	o. 2	o. 24	o. 4	o. 16	o. 10	o. 27	o. 1
p. 54	p. 1	p. 4	p. 3	p. 8	p. 9	p. 8	p. 6
q. 10	q. 4	q. 18	q. 9	q. 50	q. 7	q. 0	q. 4
r. 45	r. 5	r. 32	r. 2	r. 100	r. 3	r. 1	r. 5
s. 80	s. 1	s. 0	s. 4	s. 54	s. 5	s. 27	s. 8
t. 50	t. 2	t. 15	t. 1	t. 35	t. 4	t. 20	t. 9

Answers to Dashes 9B–12B, 9C–12C

▶ **PATH to FLUENCY** **Dashes 21–22, 19A–20A**

Complete each Dash. Check your answers on page 143.

Dash 21 **2s, 3s, 4s, 5s, 9s** **Multiplications**	**Dash 22** **2s, 3s, 4s, 5s, 9s** **Divisions**	**Dash 19A** **6s, 7s, 8s** **Multiplications**	**Dash 20A** **6s, 7s, 8s** **Divisions**
a. $6 \times 3 =$ ___	a. $16 / 4 =$ ___	a. $9 \times 6 =$ ___	a. $24 \div 6 =$ ___
b. $4 \cdot 7 =$ ___	b. $54 \div 9 =$ ___	b. $7 * 7 =$ ___	b. $21 / 7 =$ ___
c. $8 * 2 =$ ___	c. $4 / 2 =$ ___	c. $3 \cdot 7 =$ ___	c. $42 \div 7 =$ ___
d. $5 \times 3 =$ ___	d. $28 \div 4 =$ ___	d. $6 \times 3 =$ ___	d. $16 / 8 =$ ___
e. $4 \cdot 4 =$ ___	e. $25 / 5 =$ ___	e. $7 * 8 =$ ___	e. $24 \div 8 =$ ___
f. $3 \cdot 9 =$ ___	f. $21 \div 3 =$ ___	f. $8 \cdot 6 =$ ___	f. $54 / 6 =$ ___
g. $9 \times 9 =$ ___	g. $40 / 4 =$ ___	g. $5 \times 6 =$ ___	g. $36 \div 6 =$ ___
h. $8 \cdot 9 =$ ___	h. $81 \div 9 =$ ___	h. $6 * 6 =$ ___	h. $48 / 8 =$ ___
i. $6 * 4 =$ ___	i. $35 / 5 =$ ___	i. $9 \cdot 8 =$ ___	i. $49 \div 7 =$ ___
j. $3 \times 3 =$ ___	j. $12 / 3 =$ ___	j. $7 \times 6 =$ ___	j. $64 / 8 =$ ___
k. $2 \cdot 7 =$ ___	k. $2 \div 2 =$ ___	k. $2 * 7 =$ ___	k. $48 \div 6 =$ ___
l. $8 \cdot 5 =$ ___	l. $63 / 9 =$ ___	l. $4 \cdot 7 =$ ___	l. $42 / 6 =$ ___
m. $4 \times 9 =$ ___	m. $36 \div 4 =$ ___	m. $3 \times 6 =$ ___	m. $32 \div 8 =$ ___
n. $9 \cdot 5 =$ ___	n. $18 / 2 =$ ___	n. $9 * 7 =$ ___	n. $56 / 7 =$ ___
o. $7 * 3 =$ ___	o. $9 \div 3 =$ ___	o. $6 \cdot 7 =$ ___	o. $63 \div 7 =$ ___
p. $2 \times 2 =$ ___	p. $36 / 9 =$ ___	p. $6 \times 9 =$ ___	p. $72 / 8 =$ ___
q. $8 \cdot 4 =$ ___	q. $40 \div 5 =$ ___	q. $8 * 7 =$ ___	q. $30 \div 6 =$ ___
r. $5 * 1 =$ ___	r. $12 \div 4 =$ ___	r. $6 \cdot 4 =$ ___	r. $18 / 6 =$ ___
s. $5 \times 5 =$ ___	s. $9 / 9 =$ ___	s. $7 \times 3 =$ ___	s. $56 \div 8 =$ ___
t. $6 \cdot 9 =$ ___	t. $14 \div 2 =$ ___	t. $8 * 8 =$ ___	t. $28 / 7 =$ ___

Name _____   **Date** _____

► PATH to FLUENCY **Dashes 21A–22A, 19B–20B**

Complete each Dash. Check your answers on page 143.

Dash 21A 2s, 3s, 4s, 5s, 9s Multiplications	Dash 22A 2s, 3s, 4s, 5s, 9s Divisions	Dash 19B 6s, 7s, 8s Multiplications	Dash 20B 6s, 7s, 8s Divisions
a. $6 \times 9 =$ _____	a. $14 \div 2 =$ _____	a. $6 \times 2 =$ _____	a. $36 \div 6 =$ _____
b. $6 * 3 =$ _____	b. $16 / 4 =$ _____	b. $7 * 7 =$ _____	b. $63 / 7 =$ _____
c. $4 \cdot 7 =$ _____	c. $9 \div 9 =$ _____	c. $8 \cdot 5 =$ _____	c. $24 \div 8 =$ _____
d. $5 \times 5 =$ _____	d. $54 / 9 =$ _____	d. $4 \times 6 =$ _____	d. $18 / 6 =$ _____
e. $8 * 2 =$ _____	e. $12 \div 4 =$ _____	e. $3 * 7 =$ _____	e. $28 \div 7 =$ _____
f. $5 \cdot 1 =$ _____	f. $4 / 2 =$ _____	f. $1 \cdot 8 =$ _____	f. $48 / 8 =$ _____
g. $5 \times 3 =$ _____	g. $40 \div 5 =$ _____	g. $6 \times 9 =$ _____	g. $54 \div 6 =$ _____
h. $8 * 4 =$ _____	h. $28 / 4 =$ _____	h. $7 * 5 =$ _____	h. $42 / 7 =$ _____
i. $4 \cdot 4 =$ _____	i. $36 \div 9 =$ _____	i. $8 \cdot 3 =$ _____	i. $72 \div 8 =$ _____
j. $2 \times 2 =$ _____	j. $25 / 5 =$ _____	j. $4 \times 6 =$ _____	j. $6 / 6 =$ _____
k. $3 * 9 =$ _____	k. $9 \div 3 =$ _____	k. $9 * 7 =$ _____	k. $14 \div 7 =$ _____
l. $7 \cdot 3 =$ _____	l. $21 / 3 =$ _____	l. $8 \cdot 8 =$ _____	l. $56 / 8 =$ _____
m. $9 \times 9 =$ _____	m. $18 \div 2 =$ _____	m. $6 \times 1 =$ _____	m. $12 \div 6 =$ _____
n. $9 * 5 =$ _____	n. $40 / 4 =$ _____	n. $7 * 4 =$ _____	n. $7 / 7 =$ _____
o. $8 \cdot 9 =$ _____	o. $36 \div 4 =$ _____	o. $8 \cdot 6 =$ _____	o. $16 \div 8 =$ _____
p. $4 \times 9 =$ _____	p. $81 / 9 =$ _____	p. $7 \times 6 =$ _____	p. $30 / 6 =$ _____
q. $6 * 4 =$ _____	q. $63 \div 9 =$ _____	q. $2 * 7 =$ _____	q. $56 \div 7 =$ _____
r. $8 \cdot 5 =$ _____	r. $35 / 5 =$ _____	r. $9 \cdot 8 =$ _____	r. $8 / 8 =$ _____
s. $2 \times 7 =$ _____	s. $12 \div 3 =$ _____	s. $6 \times 5 =$ _____	s. $48 \div 6 =$ _____
t. $3 * 3 =$ _____	t. $2 / 2 =$ _____	t. $7 * 6 =$ _____	t. $21 / 7 =$ _____

Name _____ Date _____

► **PATH to FLUENCY** **Dashes 21B–22B, 19C–20C**

Complete each Dash. Check your answers on page 144.

Dash 21B **2s, 3s, 4s, 5s, 9s** **Multiplications**	**Dash 22B** **2s, 3s, 4s, 5s, 9s** **Divisions**	**Dash 19C** **6s, 7s, 8s** **Multiplications**	**Dash 20C** **6s, 7s, 8s** **Divisions**
a. $2 \times 3 =$ _____	a. $8 \div 2 =$ _____	a. $6 \times 8 =$ _____	a. $54 \div 6 =$ _____
b. $3 * 8 =$ _____	b. $18 / 3 =$ _____	b. $7 * 3 =$ _____	b. $49 / 7 =$ _____
c. $4 \cdot 4 =$ _____	c. $12 \div 4 =$ _____	c. $8 \cdot 6 =$ _____	c. $24 \div 8 =$ _____
d. $5 \times 6 =$ _____	d. $25 / 5 =$ _____	d. $2 \times 6 =$ _____	d. $6 / 6 =$ _____
e. $9 * 8 =$ _____	e. $63 \div 9 =$ _____	e. $8 * 7 =$ _____	e. $35 \div 7 =$ _____
f. $9 \cdot 2 =$ _____	f. $16 / 2 =$ _____	f. $9 \cdot 8 =$ _____	f. $72 / 8 =$ _____
g. $3 \times 3 =$ _____	g. $3 \div 3 =$ _____	g. $6 \times 4 =$ _____	g. $18 \div 6 =$ _____
h. $4 * 2 =$ _____	h. $28 / 4 =$ _____	h. $7 * 1 =$ _____	h. $28 / 7 =$ _____
i. $9 \cdot 5 =$ _____	i. $45 \div 5 =$ _____	i. $8 \cdot 3 =$ _____	i. $8 \div 8 =$ _____
j. $9 \times 4 =$ _____	j. $27 / 9 =$ _____	j. $5 \times 6 =$ _____	j. $30 / 6 =$ _____
k. $2 * 7 =$ _____	k. $12 \div 2 =$ _____	k. $9 * 7 =$ _____	k. $21 \div 7 =$ _____
l. $3 \cdot 5 =$ _____	l. $12 / 3 =$ _____	l. $4 \cdot 8 =$ _____	l. $40 / 8 =$ _____
m. $4 \times 8 =$ _____	m. $20 \div 4 =$ _____	m. $6 \times 6 =$ _____	m. $42 \div 6 =$ _____
n. $5 * 3 =$ _____	n. $40 / 5 =$ _____	n. $7 * 5 =$ _____	n. $63 / 7 =$ _____
o. $9 \cdot 6 =$ _____	o. $54 \div 9 =$ _____	o. $8 \cdot 8 =$ _____	o. $32 \div 8 =$ _____
p. $2 \times 8 =$ _____	p. $2 / 2 =$ _____	p. $1 \times 6 =$ _____	p. $36 / 6 =$ _____
q. $3 * 7 =$ _____	q. $9 \div 3 =$ _____	q. $2 * 7 =$ _____	q. $14 \div 7 =$ _____
r. $4 \cdot 1 =$ _____	r. $36 / 4 =$ _____	r. $5 \cdot 8 =$ _____	r. $56 / 8 =$ _____
s. $5 \times 8 =$ _____	s. $15 \div 5 =$ _____	s. $6 \times 9 =$ _____	s. $24 \div 6 =$ _____
t. $9 * 9 =$ _____	t. $9 / 9 =$ _____	t. $7 * 7 =$ _____	t. $42 / 7 =$ _____

Name   Date

► (PATH to FLUENCY) **Dashes 21C–22C, 19D–20D**

Complete each Dash. Check your answers on page 144.

Dash 21C 2s, 3s, 4s, 5s, 9s **Multiplications**	**Dash 22C** 2s, 3s, 4s, 5s, 9s **Divisions**	**Dash 19D** 6s, 7s, 8s **Multiplications**	**Dash 20D** 6s, 7s, 8s **Divisions**
a. $2 \times 9 =$ _____	a. $8 \div 2 =$ _____	a. $6 \times 9 =$ _____	a. $18 / 6 =$ _____
b. $3 * 7 =$ _____	b. $6 / 3 =$ _____	b. $7 * 6 =$ _____	b. $42 \div 7 =$ _____
c. $4 \cdot 5 =$ _____	c. $4 \div 4 =$ _____	c. $8 \cdot 2 =$ _____	c. $32 / 8 =$ _____
d. $5 \times 3 =$ _____	d. $20 / 5 =$ _____	d. $3 \times 6 =$ _____	d. $54 \div 6 =$ _____
e. $9 * 1 =$ _____	e. $63 \div 9 =$ _____	e. $4 * 7 =$ _____	e. $49 / 7 =$ _____
f. $1 \cdot 2 =$ _____	f. $16 / 2 =$ _____	f. $9 \cdot 8 =$ _____	f. $8 / 8 =$ _____
g. $4 \times 3 =$ _____	g. $15 \div 3 =$ _____	g. $6 \times 6 =$ _____	g. $30 \div 6 =$ _____
h. $4 * 1 =$ _____	h. $32 / 4 =$ _____	h. $7 * 2 =$ _____	h. $35 / 7 =$ _____
i. $7 \cdot 5 =$ _____	i. $30 \div 5 =$ _____	i. $8 \cdot 1 =$ _____	i. $48 \div 8 =$ _____
j. $9 \times 9 =$ _____	j. $45 / 9 =$ _____	j. $2 \times 6 =$ _____	j. $24 / 6 =$ _____
k. $2 * 3 =$ _____	k. $2 \div 2 =$ _____	k. $8 * 7 =$ _____	k. $14 \div 7 =$ _____
l. $3 \cdot 8 =$ _____	l. $21 / 3 =$ _____	l. $3 \cdot 8 =$ _____	l. $56 / 8 =$ _____
m. $4 \times 4 =$ _____	m. $12 \div 4 =$ _____	m. $6 \times 4 =$ _____	m. $6 \div 6 =$ _____
n. $5 * 2 =$ _____	n. $10 / 5 =$ _____	n. $7 * 5 =$ _____	n. $21 / 7 =$ _____
o. $9 \cdot 6 =$ _____	o. $9 \div 9 =$ _____	o. $8 \cdot 8 =$ _____	o. $40 \div 8 =$ _____
p. $6 \times 2 =$ _____	p. $12 / 2 =$ _____	p. $1 \times 6 =$ _____	p. $48 / 6 =$ _____
q. $9 * 3 =$ _____	q. $27 \div 3 =$ _____	q. $3 * 7 =$ _____	q. $56 \div 7 =$ _____
r. $6 \cdot 4 =$ _____	r. $20 / 4 =$ _____	r. $4 \cdot 8 =$ _____	r. $64 / 8 =$ _____
s. $5 \times 5 =$ _____	s. $40 \div 8 =$ _____	s. $6 \times 7 =$ _____	s. $36 \div 6 =$ _____
t. $3 * 9 =$ _____	t. $81 / 9 =$ _____	t. $7 * 7 =$ _____	t. $7 / 7 =$ _____

▶ Answers to Dashes 21–22, 19A–20B, 21A–22A

Use this sheet to check your answers to the Dashes on pages 139 and 140.

Dash 21 ×	Dash 22 ÷	Dash 19A ×	Dash 20A ÷	Dash 21A ×	Dash 22A ÷	Dash 19B ×	Dash 20B ÷
a. 18	a. 4	a. 54	a. 4	a. 54	a. 7	a. 12	a. 6
b. 28	b. 6	b. 49	b. 3	b. 18	b. 4	b. 49	b. 9
c. 16	c. 2	c. 21	c. 6	c. 28	c. 1	c. 40	c. 3
d. 15	d. 7	d. 18	d. 2	d. 25	d. 6	d. 24	d. 3
e. 16	e. 5	e. 56	e. 3	e. 16	e. 3	e. 21	e. 4
f. 27	f. 7	f. 48	f. 9	f. 5	f. 2	f. 8	f. 6
g. 81	g. 10	g. 30	g. 6	g. 15	g. 8	g. 54	g. 9
h. 72	h. 9	h. 36	h. 6	h. 32	h. 7	h. 35	h. 6
i. 24	i. 7	i. 72	i. 7	i. 16	i. 4	i. 24	i. 9
j. 9	j. 4	j. 42	j. 8	j. 4	j. 5	j. 24	j. 1
k. 14	k. 1	k. 14	k. 8	k. 27	k. 3	k. 63	k. 2
l. 40	l. 7	l. 28	l. 7	l. 21	l. 7	l. 64	l. 7
m. 36	m. 9	m. 18	m. 4	m. 81	m. 9	m. 6	m. 2
n. 45	n. 9	n. 63	n. 8	n. 45	n. 10	n. 28	n. 1
o. 21	o. 3	o. 42	o. 9	o. 72	o. 9	o. 48	o. 2
p. 4	p. 4	p. 54	p. 9	p. 36	p. 9	p. 42	p. 5
q. 32	q. 8	q. 56	q. 5	q. 24	q. 7	q. 14	q. 8
r. 5	r. 3	r. 24	r. 3	r. 40	r. 7	r. 72	r. 1
s. 25	s. 1	s. 21	s. 7	s. 14	s. 4	s. 30	s. 8
t. 54	t. 7	t. 64	t. 4	t. 9	t. 1	t. 42	t. 3

Name _____   Date _____

▶ Answers to Dashes 21B–22B, 19C–22C, 19D, 20D

Use this sheet to check your answers to the Dashes on pages 141 and 142.

Dash 21B ×	Dash 22B ÷	Dash 19C ×	Dash 20C ÷	Dash 21C ×	Dash 22C ÷	Dash 19D ×	Dash 20D ÷
a. 6	a. 4	a. 48	a. 9	a. 18	a. 4	a. 54	a. 3
b. 24	b. 6	b. 21	b. 7	b. 21	b. 2	b. 42	b. 6
c. 16	c. 3	c. 48	c. 3	c. 20	c. 1	c. 16	c. 4
d. 30	d. 5	d. 12	d. 1	d. 15	d. 4	d. 18	d. 9
e. 72	e. 7	e. 56	e. 5	e. 9	e. 7	e. 28	e. 7
f. 18	f. 8	f. 72	f. 9	f. 2	f. 8	f. 72	f. 1
g. 9	g. 1	g. 24	g. 3	g. 12	g. 5	g. 36	g. 5
h. 8	h. 7	h. 7	h. 4	h. 4	h. 8	h. 14	h. 5
i. 45	i. 9	i. 24	i. 1	i. 35	i. 6	i. 8	i. 6
j. 36	j. 3	j. 30	j. 5	j. 81	j. 5	j. 12	j. 4
k. 14	k. 6	k. 63	k. 3	k. 6	k. 1	k. 56	k. 2
l. 15	l. 4	l. 32	l. 5	l. 24	l. 7	l. 24	l. 7
m. 32	m. 5	m. 36	m. 7	m. 16	m. 3	m. 24	m. 1
n. 15	n. 8	n. 35	n. 9	n. 10	n. 2	n. 35	n. 3
o. 54	o. 6	o. 64	o. 4	o. 54	o. 1	o. 64	o. 5
p. 16	p. 1	p. 6	p. 6	p. 12	p. 6	p. 6	p. 8
q. 21	q. 3	q. 14	q. 2	q. 27	q. 9	q. 21	q. 8
r. 4	r. 9	r. 40	r. 7	r. 24	r. 5	r. 32	r. 8
s. 40	s. 3	s. 54	s. 4	s. 25	s. 5	s. 42	s. 6
t. 81	t. 1	t. 49	t. 6	t. 27	t. 9	t. 49	t. 1

► **PATH to FLUENCY** **What's My Rule?**

A **function table** is a table of ordered pairs. For every input number, there is only one output number. The rule describes what to do to the input number to get the output number.

Write the rule and then complete the function table.

6. Rule: _____

Input	Output
7	42
8	____
____	54
6	36

7. Rule: _____

Input	Output
81	9
45	5
72	____
____	7

8. Rule: _____

Input	Output
4	28
8	56
6	____
7	____

9. Rule: _____

Input	Output
32	8
8	2
____	3
24	____

10. Rule: _____

Input	Output
21	7
27	9
____	6
15	____

11. Rule: _____

Input	Output
5	25
____	40
9	____
3	15

► (PATH to FLUENCY) **Play *Division Three-in-a-Row***

Rules for *Division Three-in-a-Row*

Number of players: 2
What You Will Need: Division Product Cards, one
Three-in-a-Row Game Grid for each player

1. Each player writes any nine quotients in the squares
   of a game grid. A player may write the same
   quotient more than once.

2. Shuffle the cards. Place them division side up in a
   stack in the center of the table.

3. Players take turns. On each turn, a player
   completes the division on the top card and then
   partners check the answer.

4. For a correct answer, if the quotient is on the game
   grid, the player puts an X through that grid square.
   If the answer is wrong, or if the quotient is not on
   the grid, the player doesn't mark anything. The
   player puts the card division side up on the bottom
   of the stack.

5. The first player to mark three squares in a row
   (horizontally, vertically, or diagonally) wins.

2×2

$2 \cdot 3$

Hint:
What is $3 \cdot 2$?
© Houghton Mifflin Harcourt Publishing Company

$2 * 4$

Hint:
What is $4 * 2$?
© Houghton Mifflin Harcourt Publishing Company

2×5

Hint:
What is 5×2?
© Houghton Mifflin Harcourt Publishing Company

2×6

Hint:
What is 6×2?
© Houghton Mifflin Harcourt Publishing Company

$2 \cdot 7$

Hint:
What is $7 \cdot 2$?
© Houghton Mifflin Harcourt Publishing Company

$2 * 8$

Hint:
What is $8 * 2$?
© Houghton Mifflin Harcourt Publishing Company

2×9

Hint:
What is 9×2?
© Houghton Mifflin Harcourt Publishing Company

5×2

Hint:
What is 2×5?
© Houghton Mifflin Harcourt Publishing Company

$5 \cdot 3$

Hint:
What is $3 \cdot 5$?
© Houghton Mifflin Harcourt Publishing Company

$5 * 4$

Hint:
What is $4 * 5$?
© Houghton Mifflin Harcourt Publishing Company

5×5

© Houghton Mifflin Harcourt Publishing Company

5×6

Hint:
What is 6×5?
© Houghton Mifflin Harcourt Publishing Company

$5 \cdot 7$

Hint:
What is $7 \cdot 5$?
© Houghton Mifflin Harcourt Publishing Company

$5 * 8$

Hint:
What is $8 * 5$?
© Houghton Mifflin Harcourt Publishing Company

5×9

Hint:
What is 9×5?
© Houghton Mifflin Harcourt Publishing Company

Name _____ **Date** _____

$2 \overline{)10}$

Hint: What is
$\square \times 2 = 10$?

$2 \overline{)8}$

Hint: What is
$\square \times 2 = 8$?

$2 \overline{)6}$

Hint: What is
$\square \times 2 = 6$?

$2 \overline{)4}$

Hint: What is
$\square \times 2 = 4$?

$2 \overline{)18}$

Hint: What is
$\square \times 2 = 18$?

$2 \overline{)16}$

Hint: What is
$\square \times 2 = 16$?

$2 \overline{)14}$

Hint: What is
$\square \times 2 = 14$?

$2 \overline{)12}$

Hint: What is
$\square \times 2 = 12$?

$5 \overline{)25}$

Hint: What is
$\square \times 5 = 25$?

$5 \overline{)20}$

Hint: What is
$\square \times 5 = 20$?

$5 \overline{)15}$

Hint: What is
$\square \times 5 = 15$?

$5 \overline{)10}$

Hint: What is
$\square \times 5 = 10$?

$5 \overline{)45}$

Hint: What is
$\square \times 5 = 45$?

$5 \overline{)40}$

Hint: What is
$\square \times 5 = 40$?

$5 \overline{)35}$

Hint: What is
$\square \times 5 = 35$?

$5 \overline{)30}$

Hint: What is
$\square \times 5 = 30$?

Product Cards: 2s, 5s, 9s

9×2

Hint:
What is 2×9?
© Houghton Mifflin Harcourt Publishing Company

$9 \bullet 3$

Hint:
What is $3 \cdot 9$?
© Houghton Mifflin Harcourt Publishing Company

$9 * 4$

Hint:
What is $4 * 9$?
© Houghton Mifflin Harcourt Publishing Company

9×5

Hint:
What is 5×9?
© Houghton Mifflin Harcourt Publishing Company

9×6

Hint:
What is 6×9?
© Houghton Mifflin Harcourt Publishing Company

$9 \bullet 7$

Hint:
What is $7 \cdot 9$?
© Houghton Mifflin Harcourt Publishing Company

$9 * 8$

Hint:
What is $8 * 9$?
© Houghton Mifflin Harcourt Publishing Company

9×9

© Houghton Mifflin Harcourt Publishing Company

$\times$

$\bullet$

$*$

$\times$

$\times$

$\bullet$

$*$

$\times$

© Houghton Mifflin Harcourt Publishing Company

You can write any numbers on the last 8 cards. Use them to practice difficult problems or if you lose a card.

$9\overline{)45}$

Hint: What is
$\square \times 9 = 45?$
© Houghton Mifflin Harcourt Publishing Company

$9\overline{)36}$

Hint: What is
$\square \times 9 = 36?$
© Houghton Mifflin Harcourt Publishing Company

$9\overline{)27}$

Hint: What is
$\square \times 9 = 27?$
© Houghton Mifflin Harcourt Publishing Company

$9\overline{)18}$

Hint: What is
$\square \times 9 = 18?$
© Houghton Mifflin Harcourt Publishing Company

$9\overline{)81}$

Hint: What is
$\square \times 9 = 81?$
© Houghton Mifflin Harcourt Publishing Company

$9\overline{)72}$

Hint: What is
$\square \times 9 = 72?$
© Houghton Mifflin Harcourt Publishing Company

$9\overline{)63}$

Hint: What is
$\square \times 9 = 63?$
© Houghton Mifflin Harcourt Publishing Company

$9\overline{)54}$

Hint: What is
$\square \times 9 = 54?$
© Houghton Mifflin Harcourt Publishing Company

You can write any numbers on the last 8 cards. Use them to practice difficult problems or if you lose a card.

Name

Date

3×2

Hint:
What is 2×3?
© Houghton Mifflin Harcourt Publishing Company

$3 \bullet 3$

© Houghton Mifflin Harcourt Publishing Company

$3 * 4$

Hint:
What is $4 * 3$?
© Houghton Mifflin Harcourt Publishing Company

3×5

Hint:
What is 5×3?
© Houghton Mifflin Harcourt Publishing Company

3×6

Hint:
What is 6×3?
© Houghton Mifflin Harcourt Publishing Company

$3 \bullet 7$

Hint:
What is $7 \cdot 3$?
© Houghton Mifflin Harcourt Publishing Company

$3 * 8$

Hint:
What is $8 * 3$?
© Houghton Mifflin Harcourt Publishing Company

3×9

Hint:
What is 9×3?
© Houghton Mifflin Harcourt Publishing Company

4×2

Hint:
What is 2×4?
© Houghton Mifflin Harcourt Publishing Company

$4 \bullet 3$

Hint:
What is $3 \cdot 4$?
© Houghton Mifflin Harcourt Publishing Company

$4 * 4$

© Houghton Mifflin Harcourt Publishing Company

4×5

Hint:
What is 5×4?
© Houghton Mifflin Harcourt Publishing Company

4×6

Hint:
What is 6×4?
© Houghton Mifflin Harcourt Publishing Company

$4 \bullet 7$

Hint:
What is $7 \cdot 4$?
© Houghton Mifflin Harcourt Publishing Company

$4 * 8$

Hint:
What is $8 * 4$?
© Houghton Mifflin Harcourt Publishing Company

4×9

Hint:
What is 9×4?
© Houghton Mifflin Harcourt Publishing Company

Name   Date

$3\overline{)15}$ $3\overline{)12}$ $3\overline{)9}$ $3\overline{)6}$

Hint: What is
$\square \times 3 = 15$?
© Houghton Mifflin Harcourt Publishing Company

Hint: What is
$\square \times 3 = 12$?
© Houghton Mifflin Harcourt Publishing Company

Hint: What is
$\square \times 3 = 9$?
© Houghton Mifflin Harcourt Publishing Company

Hint: What is
$\square \times 3 = 6$?
© Houghton Mifflin Harcourt Publishing Company

$3\overline{)27}$ $3\overline{)24}$ $3\overline{)21}$ $3\overline{)18}$

Hint: What is
$\square \times 3 = 27$?
© Houghton Mifflin Harcourt Publishing Company

Hint: What is
$\square \times 3 = 24$?
© Houghton Mifflin Harcourt Publishing Company

Hint: What is
$\square \times 3 = 21$?
© Houghton Mifflin Harcourt Publishing Company

Hint: What is
$\square \times 3 = 18$?
© Houghton Mifflin Harcourt Publishing Company

$4\overline{)20}$ $4\overline{)16}$ $4\overline{)12}$ $4\overline{)8}$

Hint: What is
$\square \times 4 = 20$?
© Houghton Mifflin Harcourt Publishing Company

Hint: What is
$\square \times 4 = 16$?
© Houghton Mifflin Harcourt Publishing Company

Hint: What is
$\square \times 4 = 12$?
© Houghton Mifflin Harcourt Publishing Company

Hint: What is
$\square \times 4 = 8$?
© Houghton Mifflin Harcourt Publishing Company

$4\overline{)36}$ $4\overline{)32}$ $4\overline{)28}$ $4\overline{)24}$

Hint: What is
$\square \times 4 = 36$?
© Houghton Mifflin Harcourt Publishing Company

Hint: What is
$\square \times 4 = 32$?
© Houghton Mifflin Harcourt Publishing Company

Hint: What is
$\square \times 4 = 28$?
© Houghton Mifflin Harcourt Publishing Company

Hint: What is
$\square \times 4 = 24$?
© Houghton Mifflin Harcourt Publishing Company

© Houghton Mifflin Harcourt Publishing Company

Name

Date

6×2

Hint:
What is 2×6?

$6 \cdot 3$

Hint:
What is $3 \cdot 6$?

$6 * 4$

Hint:
What is $4 * 6$?

6×5

Hint:
What is 5×6?

6×6

$6 \cdot 7$

Hint:
What is $7 \cdot 6$?

$6 * 8$

Hint:
What is $8 * 6$?

6×9

Hint:
What is 9×6?

7×2

Hint:
What is 2×7?

$7 \cdot 3$

Hint:
What is $3 \cdot 7$?

$7 * 4$

Hint:
What is $4 * 7$?

7×5

Hint:
What is 5×7?

7×6

Hint:
What is 6×7?

$7 \cdot 7$

$7 * 8$

Hint:
What is $8 * 7$?

7×9

Hint:
What is 9×7?

Name _____ **Date** _____

$6\overline{)30}$

Hint: What is
$\square \times 6 = 30?$
© Houghton Mifflin Harcourt Publishing Company

$6\overline{)24}$

Hint: What is
$\square \times 6 = 24?$
© Houghton Mifflin Harcourt Publishing Company

$6\overline{)18}$

Hint: What is
$\square \times 6 = 18?$
© Houghton Mifflin Harcourt Publishing Company

$6\overline{)12}$

Hint: What is
$\square \times 6 = 12?$
© Houghton Mifflin Harcourt Publishing Company

$6\overline{)54}$

Hint: What is
$\square \times 6 = 54?$
© Houghton Mifflin Harcourt Publishing Company

$6\overline{)48}$

Hint: What is
$\square \times 6 = 48?$
© Houghton Mifflin Harcourt Publishing Company

$6\overline{)42}$

Hint: What is
$\square \times 6 = 42?$
© Houghton Mifflin Harcourt Publishing Company

$6\overline{)36}$

Hint: What is
$\square \times 6 = 36?$
© Houghton Mifflin Harcourt Publishing Company

$7\overline{)35}$

Hint: What is
$\square \times 7 = 35?$
© Houghton Mifflin Harcourt Publishing Company

$7\overline{)28}$

Hint: What is
$\square \times 7 = 28?$
© Houghton Mifflin Harcourt Publishing Company

$7\overline{)21}$

Hint: What is
$\square \times 7 = 21?$
© Houghton Mifflin Harcourt Publishing Company

$7\overline{)14}$

Hint: What is
$\square \times 7 = 14?$
© Houghton Mifflin Harcourt Publishing Company

$7\overline{)63}$

Hint: What is
$\square \times 7 = 63?$
© Houghton Mifflin Harcourt Publishing Company

$7\overline{)56}$

Hint: What is
$\square \times 7 = 56?$
© Houghton Mifflin Harcourt Publishing Company

$7\overline{)49}$

Hint: What is
$\square \times 7 = 49?$
© Houghton Mifflin Harcourt Publishing Company

$7\overline{)42}$

Hint: What is
$\square \times 7 = 42?$
© Houghton Mifflin Harcourt Publishing Company

© Houghton Mifflin Harcourt Publishing Company

Product Cards: 6s, 7s, 8s

Name

Date

8×2

Hint:
What is 2×8?
© Houghton Mifflin Harcourt Publishing Company

$8 \cdot 3$

Hint:
What is $3 \cdot 8$?
© Houghton Mifflin Harcourt Publishing Company

$8 * 4$

Hint:
What is $4 * 8$?
© Houghton Mifflin Harcourt Publishing Company

8×5

Hint:
What is 5×8?
© Houghton Mifflin Harcourt Publishing Company

8×6

Hint:
What is 6×8?
© Houghton Mifflin Harcourt Publishing Company

$8 \cdot 7$

Hint:
What is $7 \cdot 8$?
© Houghton Mifflin Harcourt Publishing Company

$8 * 8$

Hint:
What is $8 * 8$?
© Houghton Mifflin Harcourt Publishing Company

8×9

Hint:
What is 9×8?
© Houghton Mifflin Harcourt Publishing Company

$\times$

$\bullet$

$*$

$\times$

$\times$

$\bullet$

$*$

$\times$

You can write any numbers on the last 8 cards. Use them to practice difficult problems or if you lose a card.

$8\overline{)40}$

Hint: What is
$\square \times 8 = 40?$
© Houghton Mifflin Harcourt Publishing Company

$8\overline{)32}$

Hint: What is
$\square \times 8 = 32?$
© Houghton Mifflin Harcourt Publishing Company

$8\overline{)24}$

Hint: What is
$\square \times 8 = 24?$
© Houghton Mifflin Harcourt Publishing Company

$8\overline{)16}$

Hint: What is
$\square \times 8 = 16?$
© Houghton Mifflin Harcourt Publishing Company

$8\overline{)72}$

Hint: What is
$\square \times 8 = 72?$
© Houghton Mifflin Harcourt Publishing Company

$8\overline{)64}$

Hint: What is
$\square \times 8 = 64?$
© Houghton Mifflin Harcourt Publishing Company

$8\overline{)56}$

Hint: What is
$\square \times 8 = 56?$
© Houghton Mifflin Harcourt Publishing Company

$8\overline{)48}$

Hint: What is
$\square \times 8 = 48?$
© Houghton Mifflin Harcourt Publishing Company

You can write any numbers on the last 8 cards. Use them to practice difficult problems or if you lose a card.

Product Cards: 6s, 7s, 8s

Name _____ Date _____

► PATH to FLUENCY **Diagnostic Checkup for Basic Multiplication**

1. $7 \times 5 = 35$ 2. $2 \times 3 = 6$ 3. $9 \times 9 = 81$ 4. $9 \times 6 = 54$

5. $6 \times 2 = 12$ 6. $3 \times 0 = 0$ 7. $3 \times 4 = 12$ 8. $6 \times 8 = 48$

9. $5 \times 9 = 45$ 10. $3 \times 3 = 9$ 11. $2 \times 9 = 18$ 12. $5 \times 7 = 35$

13. $6 \times 10 = 60$ 14. $4 \times 1 = 4$ 15. $6 \times 4 = 24$ 16. $4 \times 8 = 32$

17. $5 \times 2 = 10$ 18. $1 \times 3 = 3$ 19. $3 \times 9 = 27$ 20. $7 \times 6 = 42$

21. $7 \times 2 = 14$ 22. $9 \times 0 = 0$ 23. $8 \times 9 = 72$ 24. $8 \times 7 = 56$

25. $8 \times 10 = 80$ 26. $6 \times 3 = 18$ 27. $4 \times 4 = 16$ 28. $3 \times 8 = 24$

29. $5 \times 5 = 25$ 30. $6 \times 0 = 0$ 31. $7 \times 9 = 63$ 32. $6 \times 6 = 36$

33. $9 \times 2 = 18$ 34. $8 \times 3 = 22$ 35. $5 \times 4 = 20$ 36. $7 \times 7 = 44$

37. $5 \times 10 = 50$ 38. $5 \times 1 = 5$ 39. $10 \times 9 = 90$ 40. $5 \times 6 = 30$

41. $6 \times 5 = 30$ 42. $9 \times 3 = 27$ 43. $4 \times 2 = 9$ 44. $7 \times 8 = 56$

45. $8 \times 2 = 16$ 46. $5 \times 0 = 0$ 47. $4 \times 9 = 36$ 48. $6 \times 7 = 42$

49. $9 \times 5 = 45$ 50. $6 \times 1 = 6$ 51. $7 \times 4 = 28$ 52. $9 \times 8 = 72$

53. $4 \times 10 = 40$ 54. $5 \times 3 = 15$ 55. $6 \times 9 = 54$ 56. $8 \times 6 = 48$

57. $8 \times 5 = 40$ 58. $8 \times 0 = 0$ 59. $8 \times 4 = 32$ 60. $4 \times 7 = 28$

61. $3 \times 5 = 15$ 62. $7 \times 3 = 21$ 63. $5 \times 9 = 45$ 64. $3 \times 6 = 18$

65. $7 \times 10 = 70$ 66. $8 \times 1 = 2$ 67. $0 \times 4 = 0$ 68. $9 \times 7 = 63$

69. $4 \times 5 = 20$ 70. $4 \times 3 = 12$ 71. $1 \times 9 = 9$ 72. $8 \times 8 = 64$

► PATH to FLUENCY **Diagnostic Checkup for Basic Division**

1. $12 \div 2 =$ ___   2. $8 \div 1 =$ ___   3. $36 \div 9 =$ ___   4. $35 \div 7 =$ ___

5. $20 \div 5 =$ ___   6. $24 \div 3 =$ ___   7. $12 \div 4 =$ ___   8. $6 \div 6 =$ ___

9. $6 \div 2 =$ ___   10. $3 \div 3 =$ ___   11. $18 \div 9 =$ ___   12. $63 \div 7 =$ ___

13. $20 \div 10 =$ ___   14. $0 \div 1 =$ ___   15. $40 \div 4 =$ ___   16. $48 \div 8 =$ ___

17. $18 \div 2 =$ ___   18. $6 \div 3 =$ ___   19. $8 \div 4 =$ ___   20. $36 \div 6 =$ ___

21. $8 \div 2 =$ ___   22. $9 \div 1 =$ ___   23. $9 \div 9 =$ ___   24. $56 \div 7 =$ ___

25. $40 \div 5 =$ ___   26. $9 \div 3 =$ ___   27. $36 \div 4 =$ ___   28. $56 \div 8 =$ ___

29. $80 \div 10 =$ ___   30. $7 \div 1 =$ ___   31. $45 \div 9 =$ ___   32. $48 \div 6 =$ ___

33. $5 \div 5 =$ ___   34. $30 \div 3 =$ ___   35. $16 \div 4 =$ ___   36. $72 \div 8 =$ ___

37. $10 \div 2 =$ ___   38. $1 \div 1 =$ ___   39. $54 \div 9 =$ ___   40. $21 \div 7 =$ ___

41. $25 \div 5 =$ ___   42. $15 \div 3 =$ ___   43. $32 \div 4 =$ ___   44. $24 \div 8 =$ ___

45. $90 \div 10 =$ ___   46. $18 \div 3 =$ ___   47. $63 \div 9 =$ ___   48. $54 \div 6 =$ ___

49. $45 \div 5 =$ ___   50. $6 \div 1 =$ ___   51. $20 \div 4 =$ ___   52. $49 \div 7 =$ ___

53. $15 \div 5 =$ ___   54. $0 \div 3 =$ ___   55. $28 \div 4 =$ ___   56. $30 \div 6 =$ ___

57. $16 \div 2 =$ ___   58. $21 \div 3 =$ ___   59. $81 \div 9 =$ ___   60. $64 \div 8 =$ ___

61. $30 \div 5 =$ ___   62. $12 \div 3 =$ ___   63. $27 \div 9 =$ ___   64. $42 \div 7 =$ ___

65. $40 \div 10 =$ ___   66. $10 \div 1 =$ ___   67. $24 \div 4 =$ ___   68. $18 \div 6 =$ ___

69. $35 \div 5 =$ ___   70. $27 \div 3 =$ ___   71. $72 \div 9 =$ ___   72. $42 \div 6 =$ ___

▶ Vocabulary

Choose the best word from the box.

1. A(n) _____ is an arrangement of objects in columns and rows. (Lesson 2-4)

2. A(n) _____ is a product of a whole number and itself. (Lesson 2-6)

3. 80 is a(n) _____ of 10. (Lesson 2-12)

▶ Concepts and Skills

4. Explain how to use the order of operations to find the answer to this expression. Then find the answer. (Lesson 2-10)

$$3 + 4 \times 5 =$$

_____

_____

_____

5. Describe how to use mental math to find 90×8. (Lesson 2-12)

_____

_____

Find the answer. (Lesson 2-10)

6. $(7 - 4) \times 5 =$ _____   7. $4 + 18 \div 3 =$ _____

Multiply or divide.

(Lessons 2-1, 2-3, 2-5, 2-6, 2-7, 2-8, 2-12, 2-14)

8. $7 \times 8 =$ ☐   9. $6 \cdot 9 =$ ☐   10. $55 \div 1 =$ ☐

11. $72 \div 9 =$ ☐   12. $30 \times 0 =$ ☐   13. $49/7 =$ ☐

14. $4 \cdot 3 =$ ☐   15. $2 * 10 =$ ☐   16. ☐ $= 8 \times 8$

Multiply or divide.

(Lessons 2-1, 2-3, 2-5, 2-6, 2-7, 2-8, 2-12, 2-14)

17. ☐ × 3 = 24   18. 28 ÷ ☐ = 4   19. 3 × 90 = ☐

20. ☐ 6)‾24‾   21. ☐ 7)‾42‾

▶ Problem Solving

Write an equation and solve the problem.

(Lessons 2-2, 2-4, 2-7, 2-9, 2-10, 2-11, 2-13, 2-15)

22. The area of Keshawn's garden is 64 square feet. Its width is 8 feet. What is the length of this garden?

_____

23. Carrie found 7 seashells at the beach. Her brother found 8 seashells. They divided the seashells equally among 3 people. How many seashells did each person get?

_____

24. Mr. Alberto has 48 students to divide into teams of 8. The number of teams will be divided equally for three high school students to coach at practice. How many teams will each high school student get?

_____

25. **Extended Response** Marci has 7 bean bag dolls. Lucy has 2 bean bag dolls. Janice has twice the number of dolls as Marci and Lucy combined. How many dolls does Janice have? Explain the steps you used to solve the problem. Then write an equation to show the steps.

_____

_____

Dear Family,

In this unit, students explore ways to measure things using the customary and metric systems of measurement.

The units of measure we will be working with include:

U.S. Customary System
Length
1 foot (ft) = 12 inches (in.)
1 yard (yd) = 3 feet (ft)
1 mile (mi) = 5,280 feet (ft)
Capacity
1 cup (c) = 8 fluid ounces (oz)
1 pint (pt) = 2 cups (c)
1 quart (qt) = 2 pints (pt)
1 gallon (gal) = 4 quarts (qt)
Weight
1 pound (lb) = 16 ounces (oz)

Metric System
Length
1 meter (m) = 10 decimeters (dm)
1 meter (m) = 100 centimeters (cm)
1 decimeter (dm) = 10 centimeters (cm)
Capacity
1 liter (L) = 1,000 milliliters (mL)
Mass
1 kilogram (kg) = 1,000 grams (g)

Students will solve problems that involve liquid volumes or masses given in the same unit by adding, subtracting, multiplying, or dividing and by using a drawing to represent the problem.

Students will also generate measurement data with halves and fourths of an inch such as hand spans and lengths of standing broad jumps and graph their data in a line plot.

You can help your child become familiar with these units of measure by working with measurements together. For example, you might estimate and measure the length of something in inches. You might use a measuring cup to explore how the cup can be used to fill pints, quarts, or gallons of liquid.

Thank you for helping your child learn important math skills. Please call if you have any questions or comments.

Sincerely,
Your child's teacher

© Houghton Mifflin Harcourt Publishing Company

This unit includes the Common Core Standards for Mathematical Content for Operations and Algebraic Thinking, CC.3.OA.3; Number and Operations in Base Ten, CC.3.NBT.2; Measurement and Data, CC.3.MD.1, CC.3.MD.2, CC.3.MD.3, CC.3.MD.4; and for all Mathematical Practices.

Estimada familia:

En esta unidad los niños estudian cómo medir cosas usando el sistema usual de medidas y el sistema métrico decimal.

Las unidades de medida con las que trabajaremos incluirán:

Sistema usual	Sistema métrico decimal
Longitud	**Longitud**
1 pie (ft) = 12 pulgadas (pulg)	1 metro (m) = 10 decímetros (dm)
1 yarda (yd) = 3 pies (ft)	1 metro (m) = 100 centímetros (cm)
1 milla (mi) = 5,280 pies (ft)	1 decímetro (dm) = 10 centímetros (cm)
Capacidad	**Capacidad**
1 taza (tz) = 8 onzas líquidas (oz)	1 litro (L) = 1,000 mililitros (mL)
1 pinta (pt) = 2 tazas (tz)	
1 cuarto (ct) = 2 pintas (pt)	
1 galón (gal) = 4 cuartos (ct)	
Peso	**Masa**
1 libra (lb) = 16 onzas (oz)	1 kilogramo (kg) = 1,000 gramos (g)

Los estudiantes resolverán problemas relacionados con volúmenes de líquido o masas, que se dan en la misma unidad, sumando, restando o dividiendo, y usando un dibujo para representar el problema.

También generarán datos de medidas, usando medios y cuartos de pulgada, de cosas tales como el palmo de una mano y la longitud de saltos largos, y representarán los datos en un diagrama de puntos.

Puede ayudar a que su niño se familiarice con estas unidades de medida midiendo con él diversas cosas. Por ejemplo, podrían estimar y medir la longitud de algo en pulgadas. Podrían usar una taza de medidas para aprender cómo se pueden llenar pintas, cuartos o galones con líquido.

Gracias por ayudar a su niño a aprender destrezas matemáticas importantes. Si tiene alguna duda o algún comentario, por favor comuníquese conmigo.

Atentamente,
El maestro de su niño

© Houghton Mifflin Harcourt Publishing Company

COMMON CORE

Esta unidad incluye los Common Core Standards for Mathematical Content for Operations and Algebraic Thinking, CC.3.OA.3; Number and Operations in Base Ten, CC.3.NBT.2; Measurement and Data, CC.3.MD.1, CC.3.MD.2, CC.3.MD.3, CC.3.MD.4; and for all Mathematical Practices.

▶ Units of Length

Circle length units and fractions of units to show the length of the **line segment**. Write the length.

1.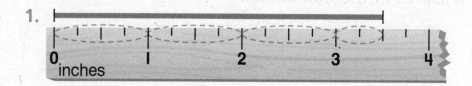

_____

2.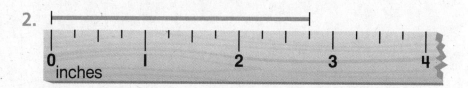

_____

3.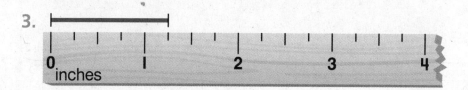

_____

4.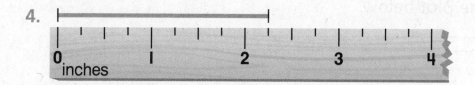

_____

5.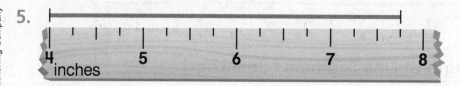

_____

6. Why is this ruler wrong?

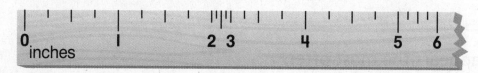

_____

_____

► Make a Line Plot

Your teacher will ask each student to read his or her actual measure for the line segments you and your classmates drew with a straightedge on Student Book page 160. Record the measures in the box below.

17. Use the measurement data from the box above to complete the line plot below.

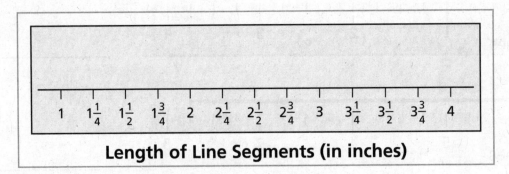

Length of Line Segments (in inches)

18. How many of the line segments have a measure of $2\frac{1}{2}$ inches?

_____

19. Which length appears the most often on the line plot?

_____

Customary Units of Length

▶ Use Drawings to Solve Problems

Use the drawing to represent and solve the problem.

14. A painter mixed 5 pints of yellow and 3 pints of blue paint to make green paint. How many pints of green paint did he make?

_____

15. Ryan bought a bottle of orange juice that had 16 fluid ounces. He poured 6 fluid ounces in a cup. How many fluid ounces are left in the bottle?

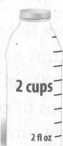

_____

16. A restaurant made 8 quarts of tea. They used all the tea to fill pitchers that hold 2 quarts each. How many pitchers were filled with tea?

_____

17. An ice cream machine makes 5 pints of ice cream in a batch. If 3 batches were made, how many pints of ice cream were made?

_____

18. Fran has a water jug that holds 24 quarts of water. She fills it with a container that holds 4 quarts. How many times must she fill the 4-quart container and pour it into the jug to fill the jug with 24 quarts?

_____

Name _____ Date _____

▶ Solve Problems

**Use the drawing to represent and
solve the problem.**

Show Your Work.

19. Shanna bought 8 juice boxes filled with
her favorite juice. Each box holds
10 fluid ounces. How many fluid ounces
of her favorite juice did Shanna buy?

_____

20. Juana filled her punch bowl with
12 cups of punch. She gave some of her
friends each a cup of punch. There are
7 cups of punch left in the bowl. How
many cups did she give to friends?

_____

21. Mrs. Chavez made 20 quarts of pickles.
She made 4 quarts each day. How many
days did it take her to make the pickles?

_____

22. The sandwich shop began the day with
24 pints of apple cider. They sold
18 pints in the morning and the rest in
the afternoon. How many pints of cider
did they sell in the afternoon?

_____

23. A mid-sized aquarium holds 25 gallons
of water and a large aquarium holds 35
gallons of water. How many gallons of
water is needed to fill both aquariums?

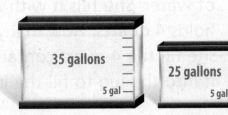

▶ Choose the Appropriate Unit

Choose the unit you would use to measure the liquid volume of each. Write _mL_ or _L_.

1. a kitchen sink _____

2. a soup spoon _____

3. a teacup _____

4. a washing machine _____

Circle the better estimate.

5. a juice container   1 L   1 mL

6. a bowl of soup   500 L   500 mL

▶ Use Drawings to Represent Problems

Use the drawing to represent and solve the problem.

7. There were 900 milliliters of water in a pitcher. Terri poured 500 milliliters of water into a bowl. How many milliliters of water are left in the pitcher?

   _____

8. Mr. Rojo put 6 liters of fuel into a gas can that can hold 10 liters. Then he added more liters to fill the can. How many liters of fuel did he add to the can?

   _____

9. Shelby needs to water each of her 3 plants with 200 milliliters of water. How many milliliters of water does she need?

   _____

Name _____   Date _____

▶ Make Sense of Problems Involving Liquid Volume

Use the drawing to represent and solve the problem.

10. The deli sold 24 liters of lemonade in 3 days. The same amount was sold each day. How many liters of lemonade did the deli sell each day?

_____

11. Tim has a bucket filled with 12 liters of water and a bucket filled with 20 liters of water. What is the total liquid volume of the buckets?

_____

12. Bella made a smoothie and gave her friend 250 milliliters. There are 550 milliliters left. How many milliliters of smoothie did Sara make?

_____

Solve. Use a drawing if you need to.

13. Diane has 36 cups of lemonade to divide equally among 4 tables. How many cups should she put at each table?

14. Mr. Valle filled 7 jars with his famous barbeque sauce. Each jar holds 2 pints. How many pints of sauce did he have?

VOCABULARY
weight
pound (lb)
ounce (oz)

▶ Choose the Appropriate Unit

Choose the unit you would use to measure the weight of each. Write *pound or ounce*.

1. a backpack full of books

   _____

2. a couch

   _____

3. a peanut

   _____

4. a pencil

   _____

Circle the better estimate.

5. a student desk   3 lb   30 lb

6. a television   20 oz   20 lb

7. a hamster   5 oz   5 lb

8. a slice of cheese   1 lb   1 oz

▶ Use Drawings to Represent Problems

Use the drawing to represent and solve the problem.

9. Selma filled each of 3 bags with 5 ounces of her favorite nuts. How many ounces of nuts did she use altogether to fill the bags?

   _____

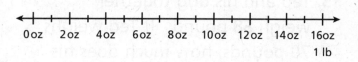

10. Two apples together weigh 16 ounces. If one apple weighs 9 ounces, how much does the other apple weigh?

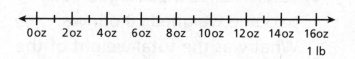

▶ Use Drawings to Represent Problems (continued)

Use the drawing to represent and solve the problem.

11. Noah bought 16 ounces of turkey meat. If he uses 4 ounces to make a turkey patty, how many patties can he make?

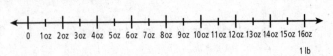

_____

12. A package of silver beads weighs 6 ounces and a package of wooden beads weighs 7 ounces more. How much does the package of wooden beads weigh?

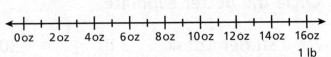

_____

▶ Solve Word Problems

Solve. Use a drawing if you need to.

13. Ted and his dog together weigh 88 pounds. If Ted weighs 70 pounds, how much does his dog weigh?

_____

14. Emma has 20 ounces of popcorn kernels in a bag. If she pops 4 ounces of kernels at a time, how many times can Emma pop corn?

_____

15. Susan mailed 3 packages. Each package weighed 20 ounces. What was the total weight of the 3 packages?

_____

16. Bailey caught two fish. The smaller fish weighs 14 ounces and the larger fish weighs 6 ounces more. How much does the larger fish weigh?

_____

Customary Units of Weight and Metric Units of Mass

► Choose the Appropriate Unit

Choose the unit you would use to measure the mass of each. Write *gram* or *kilogram*.

17. an elephant

_____

18. a crayon

_____

19. a stamp

_____

20. a dog

_____

Circle the better estimate.

21. a pair of sunglasses   150 g   150 kg

22. a horse   6 kg   600 kg

23. a watermelon   40 g   4 kg

24. a quarter   500 g   5 g

► Use Drawings to Represent Problems

Use the drawing to represent and solve the problem.

25. Zach wants to buy 900 grams of pumpkin seed. The scale shows 400 grams. How many more grams does he need?

_____

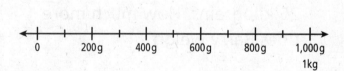

26. Laura had 800 grams of fruit snacks. She put an equal amount into each of 4 containers. How many grams did she put in each container?

_____

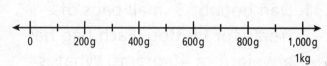

► Solve Word Problems

Use the drawing to represent and solve the problem.

27. Nancy used 30 grams of strawberries and 45 grams of apples in her salad. How many grams of fruit altogether did she put in her salad?

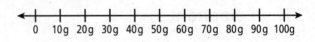

_____

28. Three people each donated a 20-kilogram bag of dog food to the animal shelter. How many kilograms of dog food was donated altogether?

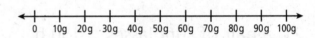

_____

Solve. Use a drawing if you need to.

29. Barry weighs 40 kilograms and his younger brother weighs 25 kilograms. How much more does Barry weigh?

_____

30. Jolie made 3 necklaces that have a total weight of 180 grams. If each necklace weighs the same, how much would each necklace weigh?

_____

31. Dan bought 6 small bags of treats for his dog. Each bag has a weight of 40 grams. What is the total weight of all the bags?

_____

32. Carrie has a dog and a cat. Together they have a mass of 21 kilograms. If the cat has a mass of 9 kilograms, what is the mass of Carrie's dog?

_____

Dear Family,

In math class, your child is beginning lessons about time. This topic is directly connected to home and community and involves skills your child will use often in everyday situations.

Students are reading time to the hour, half-hour, quarter-hour, five minutes, and minute, as well as describing the time before the hour and after the hour.

For example, you can read 3:49 both as after and before the hour.

Forty-nine minutes after three

Eleven minutes before four

Students will be using clocks to solve problems about elapsed time.

Help your child read time and find elapsed time. Ask your child to estimate how long it takes to do activities such as eating a meal, traveling to the store, or doing homework. Have your child look at the clock when starting an activity and then again at the end of the activity. Ask how long the activity took.

Your child will also learn to add and subtract time on a number line.

If you have any questions or comments, please call or write to me.

Sincerely,
Your child's teacher

This unit includes the Common Core Standards for Mathematical Content for Operations and Algebraic Thinking, CC.3.OA.3; Number and Operations in Base Ten, CC.3.NBT.2; Measurement and Data, CC.3.MD.1, CC.3.MD.2, CC.3.MD.3, CC.3.MD.4; and for all Mathematical Practices.

Estimada familia:

En la clase de matemáticas su niño está comenzando lecciones que le enseñan sobre la hora. Este tema se relaciona directamente con la casa y la comunidad, y trata de destrezas que su niño usará a menudo en situaciones de la vida diaria.

Los estudiantes leerán la hora, la media hora, el cuarto de hora, los cinco minutos y el minuto; también describirán la hora antes y después de la hora en punto.

Por ejemplo, 3:49 se puede leer de dos maneras:

Las tres y cuarenta y nueve   Once para las cuatro

Los estudiantes usarán relojes para resolver problemas acerca del tiempo transcurrido en diferentes situaciones.

Ayude a su niño a leer la hora y hallar el tiempo transcurrido. Pídale que estime cuánto tiempo tomarán ciertas actividades, tales como comer una comida completa, ir a la tienda o hacer la tarea. Pida a su niño que vea el reloj cuando comience la actividad y cuando la termine. Pregúntele cuánto tiempo tomó la actividad.

Su niño también aprenderá a sumar y restar tiempo en una recta numérica.

Si tiene alguna pregunta o algún comentario, por favor comuníquese conmigo.

Atentamente,
El maestro de su niño

COMMON CORE

Esta unidad incluye los Common Core Standards for Mathematical Content for Operations and Algebraic Thinking, CC.3.OA.3; Number and Operations in Base Ten, CC.3.NBT.2; Measurement and Data, CC.3.MD.1, CC.3.MD.2, CC.3.MD.3, CC.3.MD.4; and for all Mathematical Practices.

Name _____   Date _____

► Make an Analog Clock

Attach the clock hands to the clock face using a prong fastener.

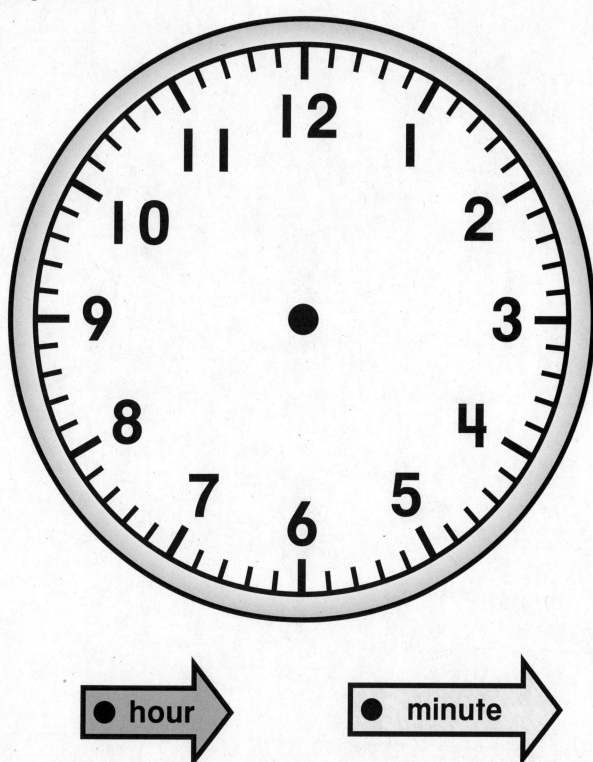

Paper Clock

▶ **Show Time to 15 Minutes**

Draw the hands on the analog clock. Write the time on the digital clock.

13. nine fifteen   **14.** half past seven   **15.** three o'clock

16. seven thirty   **17.** one forty-five   **18.** fifteen minutes after two

▶ **Times of Daily Activities**

19. Complete the table.

Time	Light or Dark	Part of the Day	Activity
3:15 A.M.			
8:00 A.M.			
2:30 P.M.			
6:15 P.M.			
8:45 P.M.			

► **Add Time**

Solve using a number line.   *Show your work.*

1. Keisha went into a park at 1:30 P.M. She hiked for 1 hour
   35 minutes. Then she went to the picnic area for 45 minutes
   and left the park. What time did Keisha leave the park?

1:30 P.M.

2. Loren arrived at the children's museum at 1:15 P.M. First,
   he spent 30 minutes looking at the dinosaur exhibit.
   Next, he watched a movie for 20 minutes. Then he spent
   15 minutes in the museum gift shop. What time did Loren
   leave the museum? How long was he in the museum?

3. Caleb started working in the yard at 8:45 A.M. He raked for
   1 hour 45 minutes and mowed for 45 minutes. Then he
   went inside. What time did he go inside? How long did
   he work in the yard?

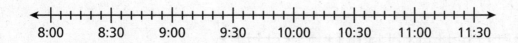

▶ **Subtract Time**

Solve using a number line.

4. Hank finished bowling at 7:15 P.M. He bowled for 2 hours 35 minutes. At what time did he start bowling?

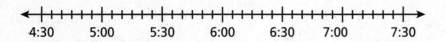

5. Miguel has a job walking dogs. He finished walking the dogs at 7:10 P.M. He walked the dogs for 2 hours and 40 minutes. What time did Miguel start walking the dogs?

6. The school music program ended at 8:35 P.M. It lasted for 1 hour 50 minutes. What time did the program start?

7. Lia took bread out of the oven at 3:15 P.M. It baked for 35 minutes. She spent 15 minutes measuring the ingredients and 15 minutes mixing the batter. What time did Lia start making the bread?

Add and Subtract Time

Dear Family,

In the rest of the lessons in this unit, your child will be learning to show information in various ways. Students will learn to read and create pictographs and bar graphs. They will organize and display data in frequency tables and line plots. Students will also learn how to use graphs to solve real world problems.

Examples of pictographs, bar graphs, and line plots are shown below.

Birthday Cards Received

Bethany	✉ ✉ ✉ ✉
Raul	✉ ✉ ✉
Moishe	✉ ✉
Kirsten	✉ ✉ ✉ ◁

Each ✉ stands for 4 cards.

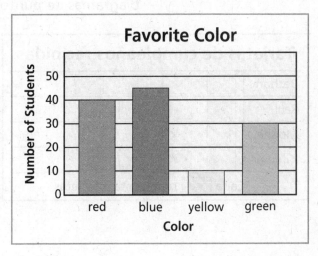

Favorite Color

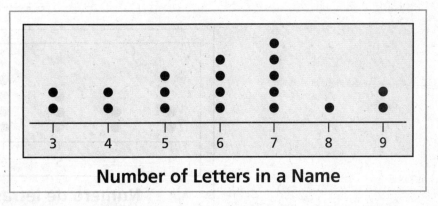

Number of Letters in a Name

Your child is learning how graphs are used in the world around us. You can help your child learn by sharing graphs that appear in newspapers, magazines, or online.

Thank you for helping your child learn how to read, interpret, and create graphs.

Sincerely,
Your child's teacher

COMMON CORE This unit includes the Common Core Standards for Mathematical Content for Operations and Algebraic Thinking, CC.3.OA.3; Number and Operations in Base Ten, CC.3.NBT.2; Measurement and Data, CC.3.MD.1, CC.3.MD.2, CC.3.MD.3, CC.3.MD.4; and for all Mathematical Practices.

Estimada familia:

Durante el resto de las lecciones de esta unidad, su niño aprenderá a mostrar información de varias maneras. Los estudiantes aprenderán a leer y a crear pictografías y gráficas de barras. Organizarán y mostrarán datos en tablas de frecuencia y en diagramas de puntos. También aprenderán cómo usar las gráficas para resolver problemas cotidianos.

Debajo se muestran ejemplos de pictografías, gráficas de barras y diagramas de puntos.

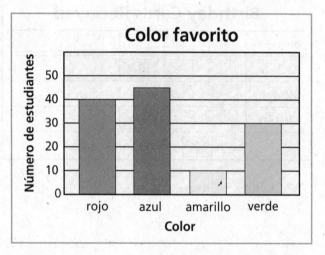

Número de letras en un nombre

Su niño está aprendiendo cómo se usan las gráficas en la vida cotidiana. Puede ayudarlo mostrándole gráficas que aparezcan en periódicos, revistas o Internet.

Gracias por ayudar a su niño a aprender cómo leer, interpretar y crear gráficas.

Atentamente,
El maestro de su niño

COMMON CORE Esta unidad incluye los Common Core Standards for Mathematical Content for Operations and Algebraic Thinking, CC.3.OA.3; Number and Operations in Base Ten, CC.3.NBT.2; Measurement and Data, CC.3.MD.1, CC.3.MD.2, CC.3.MD.3, CC.3.MD.4; and for all Mathematical Practices.

► Make a Pictograph

7. **Use the data about Kanye's CDs to make your own pictograph.**

Kanye's CDs	
Type	Number of CDs
Jazz	12
Rap	16
Classical	4

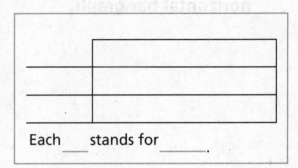

Each ___ stands for _____.

8. How many CDs in all does Kanye have?

_____

9. How many more rap CDs does Kanye have than classical?

_____

10. How many fewer jazz CDs does Kanye have than rap?

_____

11. How many pictures would you draw to show that Kanye has 9 Country and Western CDs?

_____

► **Create Bar Graphs**

16. Use the information in this table to complete the horizontal bar graph.

Favorite Way to Exercise	
Activity	Number of Students
Biking	12
Swimming	14
Walking	10

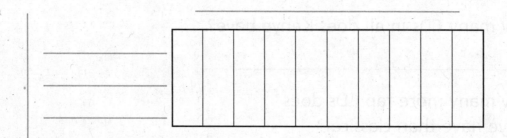

17. Use the information in this table to complete the vertical bar graph.

Favorite Team Sport	
Sport	Number of Students
Baseball	35
Soccer	60
Basketball	40

Read and Create Pictographs and Bar Graphs

► **Create Bar Graphs with Multidigit Numbers**

13. Use the information in this table to make a horizontal bar graph.

Joe's DVD Collection	
Type	**DVDs**
Comedy	60
Action	35
Drama	20

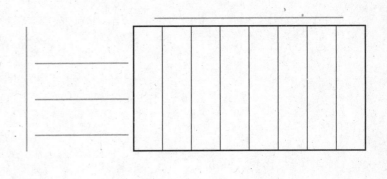

14. Use the information in this table to make a vertical bar graph.

Summer Bike Sales	
Type of Bike	**Number Sold**
Road Bike	200
Mountain Bike	600
Hybrid Bike	450

Read and Create Bar Graphs with Multidigit Numbers

▶ Create Line Plots with Fractions

1. Measure the length of the hand spans of 10 classmates to the nearest $\frac{1}{2}$ inch. Have your classmates spread their fingers apart as far as possible, and measure from the tip of the thumb to the tip of the little finger. Record the data in the tally chart below and then make a frequency table.

Tally Chart	
Length	**Tally**

Frequency Table	
Length	**Tally**

2. Use the data to make a line plot.

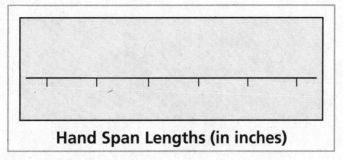

Hand Span Lengths (in inches)

3. Which length occurred the most often?

_____

4. Write a question that can be answered by using the data in the line plot.

_____

_____

Represent and Organize Data

▶ Math and Sports

Many students take part in a track and field day at school each year. One event is the standing broad jump. In the standing broad jump, the jumper stands directly behind a starting line and then jumps. The length of the jump is measured from the starting line to the mark of the first part of the jumper to touch the ground.

Complete.

1. Your teacher will tell you when to do a standing broad jump. Another student should measure the length of your jump to the nearest $\frac{1}{2}$ foot and record it on a slip of paper.

2. Record the lengths of the students' jumps in the box below.

► How Far Can a Third Grader Jump?

To analyze how far a third grader can jump, the data needs to be organized and displayed.

3. Use the lengths of the students' jumps to complete the tally chart and the frequency table.

Tally Chart	
Length	Tally

Frequency Table	
Length	Tally

4. Make a line plot.

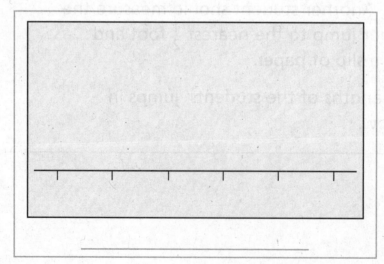

Focus on Mathematical Practices

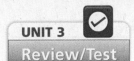
© Houghton Mifflin Harcourt Publishing Company

> **VOCABULARY**
> elapsed time
> liquid volume
> mass
> bar graph
> line plot

► Vocabulary

Choose the best word from the box.

1. You can use a _____ to show data on a number line. **(Lesson 3-1)**

2. The amount of water in a bottle can be measured with a unit of _____. **(Lesson 3-2)**

3. The time that passes between the beginning and the end of an activity is _____. **(Lesson 3-8)**

► Concepts and Skills

4. If the hour hand is half-way between the 3 and 4 on a clock in the afternoon, what time is it? Explain. **(Lesson 3-6)**

_____

_____

5. When would you use kilograms to measure something. **(Lesson 3-4)**

_____

_____

6. Estimate the length of the marker in inches. Then measure it to the nearest $\frac{1}{4}$ inch. **(Lesson 3-1)**

Estimate: _____   Actual: _____

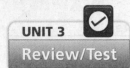
Write each time on the digital clock. Then write how to say the time. (Lessons 3-6, 3-7)

7.

┌─────────┐
│   :   │
└─────────┘

_____

8.

┌─────────┐
│   :   │
└─────────┘

_____

Circle the better estimate. (Lessons 3-2, 3-3, 3-4)

9.

2 gallons
2 cups

10.

3 milliliters
3 liters

11.

2 kilograms
2 grams

Use the table for Exercises 12 and 13. (Lessons 3-11, 3-12)

T-Shirt Sales			
Size	Small	Medium	Large
Number Sold	40	70	50

12. Use the data in the table to complete the pictograph.

T-Shirt Sales	
Small	
Medium	
Large	
Key: _____	

13. Use the data in the table to complete the bar graph.

► **Problem Solving**

Use the bar graph below to solve problems 14 and 15. (Lessons 3-11, 3-12)

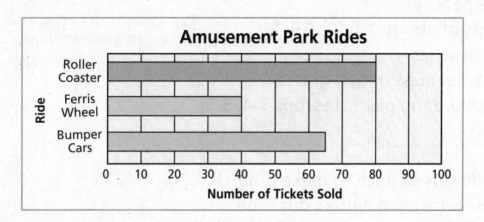

Amusement Park Rides

14. How many more tickets were
    sold for the roller coaster than
    bumper cars?

    _____

15. How many tickets were sold
    altogether?

    _____

Solve.

16. Kyle started his homework at 6:30 P.M. He spent
    35 minutes on math and 40 minutes on a science report.
    What time did he finish his homework? How long did
    he spend doing homework? (Lessons 3-9, 3-10)

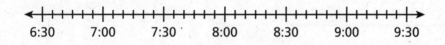

    6:30   7:00   7:30   8:00   8:30   9:00   9:30

    _____

17. At 6:45 Rico went to basketball practice. His practice
    lasted 1 hour and 20 minutes. What time did he
    finish practice? (Lesson 3-8)

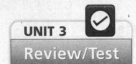
▶ Problem Solving

Use the drawing to represent and solve the problem.

18. Ariel picked some peaches.
A peach has a mass of about
150 grams. If the peaches
she picked had a total mass of 600 grams,
how many peaches did she pick? **(Lessons 3-4, 3-5)**

0   100g 200g 300g 400g 500g 600g 700g 800g 900g1000g

1kg

_____

19. Sue needs 100 milliliters of juice to make a batch
of a juice drink. How many milliliters does she
need to make 5 batches? **(Lessons 3-3, 3-5)**

1 liter

100 mL

_____

20. **Extended Response** A high school student
measured the length of third graders' feet
for a science project. The results are in the
frequency table below. Use the frequency
table to complete the line plot.
(Lessons 3-1, 3-3, 3-13, 3-14, 3-15)

What is the length of a typical third
grader's foot in this survey? Explain
why you chose that length.

_____

_____

Frequency Table								
Length (in inches)	4	$4\frac{1}{4}$	$4\frac{1}{2}$	$4\frac{3}{4}$	5	$5\frac{1}{4}$	$5\frac{1}{2}$	$5\frac{3}{4}$	6
Number of Third Graders	1	0	3	5	4	2	1	1	1

line plot

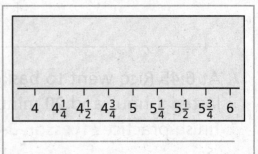

4   $4\frac{1}{4}$ $4\frac{1}{2}$ $4\frac{3}{4}$ 5 $5\frac{1}{4}$ $5\frac{1}{2}$ $5\frac{3}{4}$ 6

Dear Family,

Your child is currently participating in math activities that help him or her to understand place value, rounding, and addition and subtraction of 3-digit numbers.

- **Place Value Drawings:** Students learn to represent numbers with drawings that show how many hundreds, tens, and ones are in the numbers. Hundreds are represented by boxes. Tens are represented by vertical line segments, called ten sticks. Ones are represented by small circles. The drawings are also used to help students understand regrouping in addition and subtraction. Here is a place value drawing for the number 178.

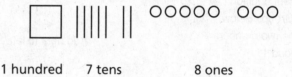

1 hundred   7 tens   8 ones

The 7 ten sticks and 8 circles are grouped in 5s so students can see the quantities easily and avoid errors.

- **Secret Code Cards:** Secret Code Cards are a set of cards for hundreds, tens, and ones. Students learn about place value by assembling the cards to show two- and three-digit numbers. Here is how the number 148 would be assembled.

| Hundreds card | Tens card | Ones card | Assembled cards |

Estimate Sums and Differences Students learn to estimate sums and differences by rounding numbers. They also use estimates to check that their actual answers are reasonable.

	Rounded to the nearest hundred	Rounded to the nearest ten
493	500	490
129	100	130
+ 369	+ 400	+ 370
991	Estimate: 1,000	Estimate: 990

Addition Methods: Students may use the common U.S. method, referred to as the New Groups Above Method, as well as two alternative methods. In the New Groups Below Method, students add from right to left and write the new ten and new hundred on the line. In the Show All Totals method, students add in either direction, write partial sums and then add the partial sums to get the total. Students also use proof drawings to demonstrate grouping 10 ones to make a new ten and grouping 10 tens to make a new hundred.

The New Groups Below Method shows the teen number 13 better than does the New Groups Above Method, where the 1 and 3 are separated. Also, addition is easier in New Groups Below, where you add the two numbers you see and just add 1.

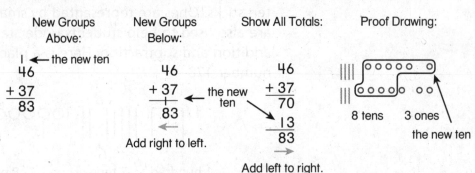

New Groups Above:

1 ← the new ten
46
+ 37
83

New Groups Below:

46
+ 37
  1
83
←
Add right to left.
the new ten

Show All Totals:

46
+ 37
70
13
83
→
Add left to right.

Proof Drawing:

8 tens   3 ones
the new ten

Subtraction Methods: Students may use the common U.S. method in which the subtraction is done right to left, with the ungrouping done before each column is subtracted. They also learn an alternative method in which all the ungrouping is done *before* the subtracting. If they do all the ungrouping first, students can subtract either from left to right or from right to left.

The Ungroup First Method helps students avoid the common error of subtracting a smaller top number from a larger bottom number.

1. Ungroup first
2. Subtract (from left to right or from right to left).

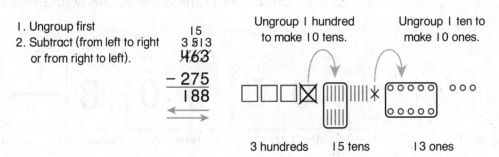

   15
  3 5 13
  4̶6̶3̶
 − 275
  188
←

Ungroup 1 hundred to make 10 tens.

Ungroup 1 ten to make 10 ones.

3 hundreds   15 tens   13 ones

Please call if you have any questions or comments.

Thank you.

Sincerely,
Your child's teacher

COMMON CORE   This unit includes the Common Core Standards for Mathematical Content for Operations and Algebraic Thinking, 3.OA.8; Number and Operation in Base Ten, 3.NBT.1 and 3.NBT.2 and all Mathematical Practices.

Estimada familia:

Su niño está participando en actividades matemáticas que le servirán para comprender el valor posicional, el redondeo y la suma y resta de números de 3 dígitos.

- **Dibujos de valor posicional:** Los estudiantes aprenden a representar números por medio de dibujos que muestran cuántas centenas, decenas y unidades contienen. Las centenas están representadas con casillas, las decenas con segmentos verticales, llamados palitos de decenas, y las unidades con círculos pequeños. Los dibujos también se usan para ayudar a los estudiantes a comprender cómo se reagrupa en la suma y en la resta. Este es un dibujo de valor posicional para el número 178.

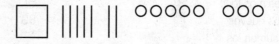

1 centena	7 decenas	8 unidades

Los palitos de decenas y los círculos se agrupan en grupos de 5 para que las cantidades se puedan ver más fácilmente y se eviten errores.

- **Tarjetas de código secreto:** Las tarjetas de código secreto son un conjunto de tarjetas con centenas, decenas y unidades. Los estudiantes aprenden acerca del valor posicional organizando las tarjetas de manera que muestren números de dos y de tres dígitos. Así se puede formar el número 148:

Tarjeta de centenas	Tarjeta de decenas	Tarjeta de unidades	Tarjetas organizadas

Estimar sumas y diferencias: Los estudiantes aprenden a estimar sumas y diferencias redondeando números. También usan las estimaciones para comprobar que sus respuestas son razonables.

	Redondear a la centena más próxima	Redondear a la decena más próxima
493	500	490
129	100	130
+ 369	+ 400	+ 370
991	Estimación: 1,000	Estimación: 990

Métodos de suma: Los estudiantes pueden usar el método común de EE. UU., conocido como Grupos nuevos arriba, y otros dos métodos alternativos. En el método de Grupos nuevos abajo, los estudiantes suman de derecha a izquierda y escriben la nueva decena y la nueva centena en el renglón. En el método de Mostrar todos los totales, los estudiantes suman en cualquier dirección, escriben sumas parciales y luego las suman para obtener el total. Los estudiantes también usan dibujos de comprobación para demostrar cómo se agrupan 10 unidades para formar una nueva decena, y 10 decenas para formar una nueva centena.

El método de Grupos nuevos abajo muestra el número 13 mejor que el método de Grupos nuevos arriba, en el que se separan los números 1 y 3. Además, es más fácil sumar con Grupos nuevos abajo, donde se suman los dos números que se ven y simplemente se añade 1.

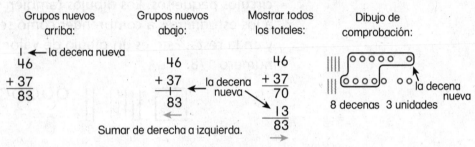

Métodos de resta: Los estudiantes pueden usar el método común de EE. UU., en el cual la resta se hace de derecha a izquierda, desagrupando antes de restar cada columna. También aprenden un método alternativo en el que desagrupan todo *antes* de restar. Si los estudiantes desagrupan todo primero, pueden restar de izquierda a derecha o de derecha a izquierda.

El método de Desagrupar primero ayuda a los estudiantes a evitar el error común de restar un número pequeño de arriba, de un número más grande de abajo.

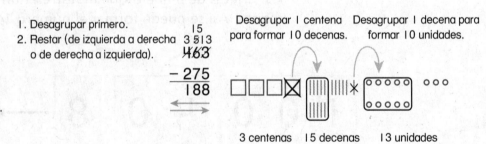

Si tiene alguna pregunta o algún comentario, por favor comuníquese conmigo. Gracias.

Atentamente,
El maestro de su niño

COMMON CORE   Esta unidad incluye los Common Core Standards for Mathematical Content for Operations and Algebraic Thinking, 3.OA.8; Number and Operation in Base Ten, 3.NBT.1 and 3.NBT.2 and all Mathematical Practices.

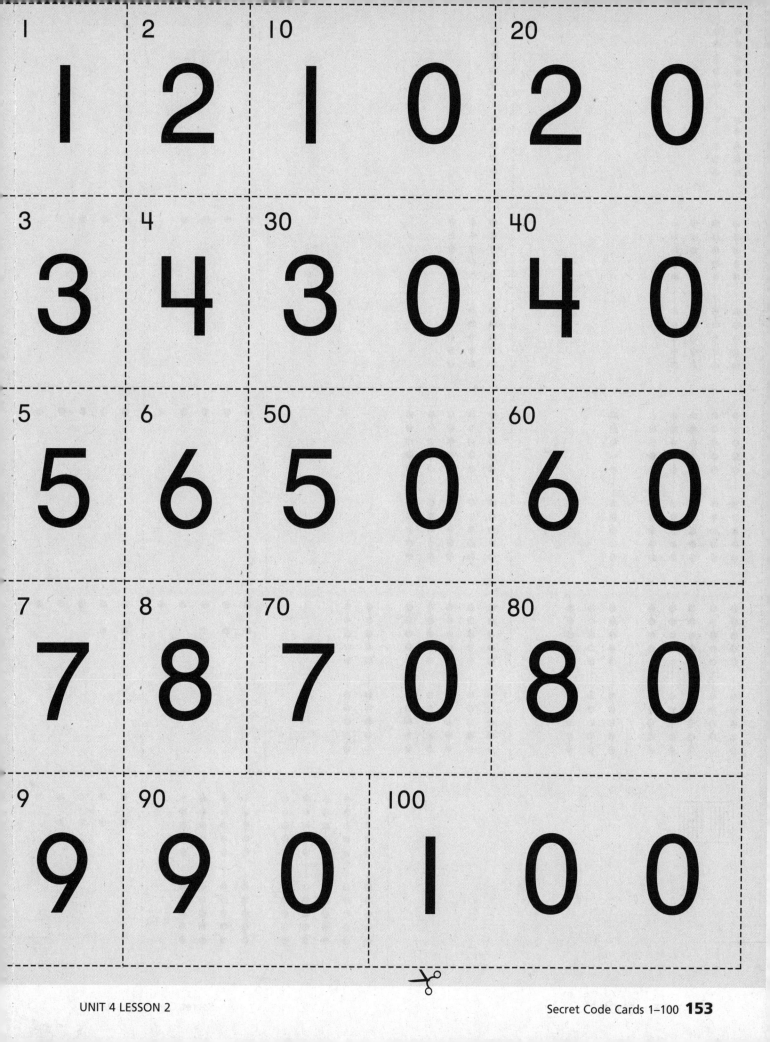

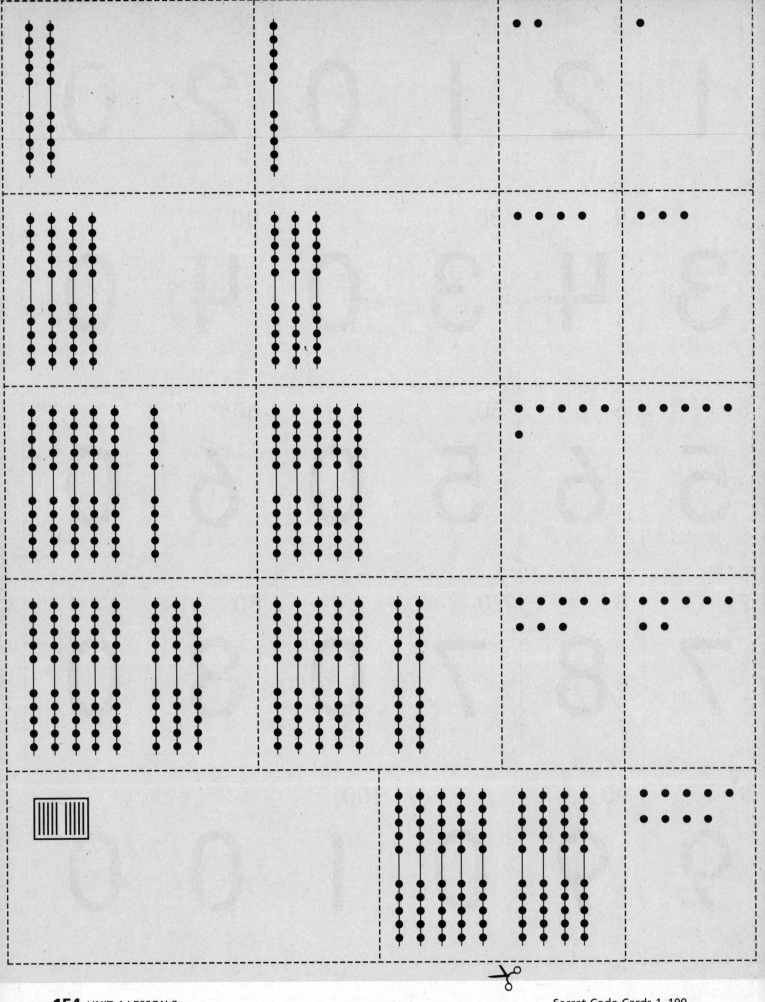

Secret Code Cards 1–100

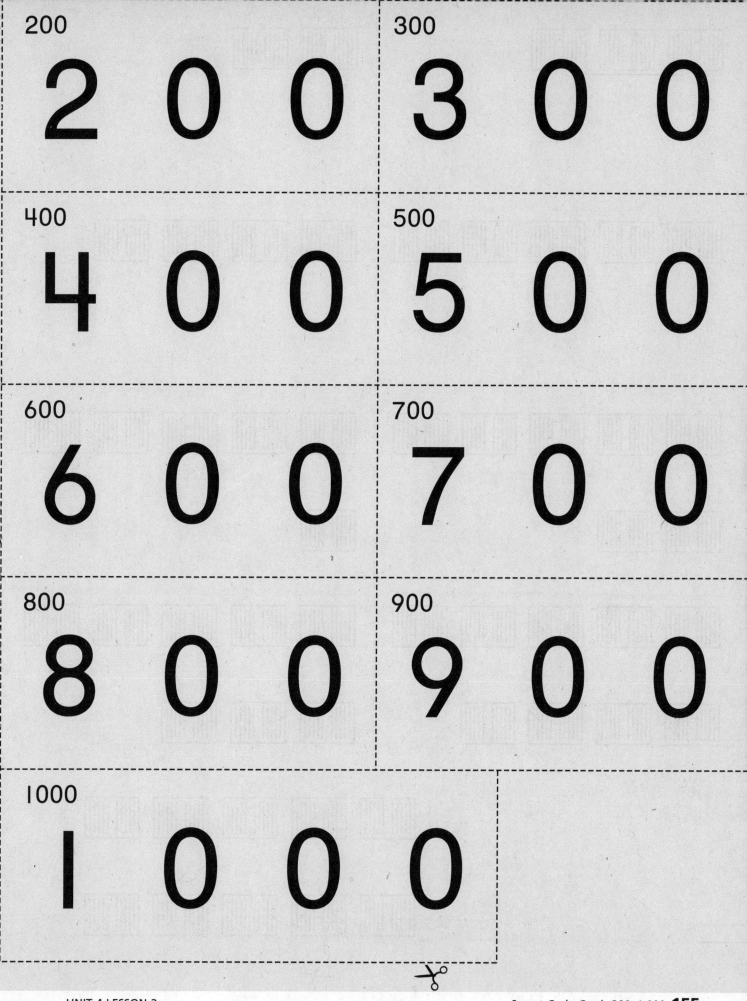

200   2 0 0

300   3 0 0

400   4 0 0

500   5 0 0

600   6 0 0

700   7 0 0

800   8 0 0

900   9 0 0

1000   1 0 0 0

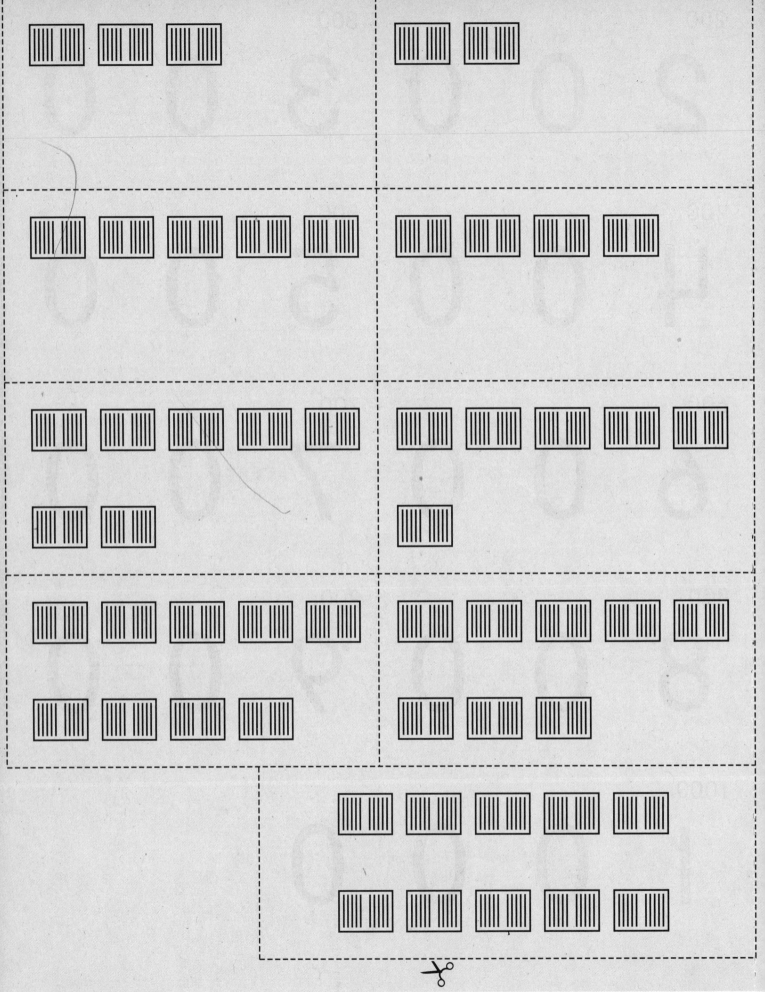

Name ______________________ Date ______________

VOCABULARY
estimate
subtract
hundreds
thousands

► Vocabulary

Choose the best word from the box.

1. When you __________ 100 from 400, the difference is 300. (Lesson 4-11)

2. The number 732 is equal to 6 __________, 13 tens, and 2 ones. (Lesson 4-1)

3. To find an answer that is close to the exact answer, you can __________. (Lesson 4-5)

► Concepts and Skills

4. Make a place value drawing to show how to add 285 and 176. (Lesson 4-7)

$$\begin{array}{r} 285 \\ +\ 176 \\ \hline \end{array}$$

5. Explain how to estimate the sum of 654 and 142 by rounding to the nearest hundred. (Lessons 4-5, 4-6)

____

____

____

____

6. Explain where and how to ungroup to do this subtraction. (Lessons 4-11, 4-12)

$$\begin{array}{r} 768 \\ -\ 575 \\ \hline \end{array}$$

____

____

Add or subtract.

(Lessons 4-1, 4-2, 4-3, 4-4, 4-7, 4-8, 4-9, 4-10, 4-11,
4-12, 4-13, 4-15, 4-16, 4-18)

7. 772
  + 129
	8. 617
	  − 549
		9. 457
		  + 123
			10. 800
			  − 684

11. 329
  + 598
	12. 831
	  + 129
		13. 900
		  − 754
			14. 267
			  − 125

15. $531 - 32 =$ 16. $713 + 88 =$ 17. $604 - 138 =$

► Problem Solving

Solve. (Lessons 4-6, 4-9, 4-10, 4-14, 4-17)

18. Gordon baked 346 blueberry muffins and 287 bran muffins, How many muffins did he bake in all?

_____

19. Write a subtraction word problem related to the addition problem in Problem 18. Then find the answer without doing any calculations.

_____

_____

20. **Extended Response** Veronica has 425 baseball cards. She gave 125 of them to her brother. Veronica's cousin gave her 285 baseball cards. Veronica says she now has 833 baseball cards. Is her answer reasonable? Explain. Then find the actual answer to check if you are correct.

_____

_____

Dear Family,

In this unit, your child will solve addition, subtraction, multiplication, and division problems involving unknown addends and factors.

- If one of the addends is unknown, it can be found by subtracting the known addend from the total or by counting on from the known addend to the total.
- If the total is unknown, it can be found by adding the addends.
- If one of the factors is unknown, it can be found by dividing the product by the other factor.
- If the product is unknown, it can be found by multiplying the factors.

Math Mountains are used to show a total and two addends. Students can use the Math Mountain to write an equation and then solve the equation to find the unknown.

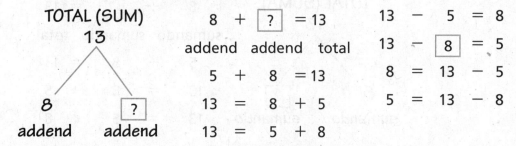

$$8 + \boxed{?} = 13 \qquad 13 - 5 = 8$$

addend addend total

$$13 - \boxed{8} = 5$$

$$5 + 8 = 13 \qquad 8 = 13 - 5$$

$$13 = 8 + 5 \qquad 5 = 13 - 8$$

$$13 = 5 + 8$$

TOTAL (SUM)
13

8 addend   ? addend

Equations with numbers alone on the left are also emphasized to help with the understanding of algebra.

Comparison Bars are used to solve problems that involve one amount that is more than or less than another amount. Drawing Comparison Bars can help a student organize the information in the problem in order to find the unknown smaller amount, the unknown larger amount, or the difference.

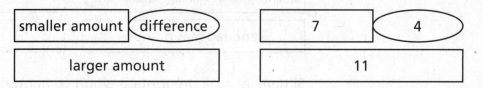

smaller amount	difference
larger amount	

7	4
11	

Please call or write if you have any questions or comments.

Sincerely,
Your child's teacher

COMMON CORE

This unit includes the Common Core Standards for Mathematical Content for Operations and Algebraic Thinking, CC.3.OA.3, CC.3.OA.4, CC.3.OA.8; Numbers and Operations in Base Ten, CC.3.NBT.1, CC.3.NBT.2, CC.3.NBT.3 and for all Mathematical Practices.

Estimada familia:

En esta unidad, su niño resolverá sumas, restas, multiplicaciones y divisiones con sumandos o factores desconocidos.

- Si uno de los sumandos se desconoce, puede hallarse restando el sumando conocido del total, o contando hacia adelante desde el sumando conocido hasta llegar al total.
- Si el total se desconoce, puede hallarse sumando los sumandos.
- Si uno de los factores se desconoce, puede hallarse dividiendo el producto entre el otro factor.
- Si el producto se desconoce, puede hallarse multiplicando los factores.

Para mostrar un total y dos sumandos se usan las **Montañas matemáticas**. Los estudiantes puede usarlas para escribir una ecuación, y al resolverla, hallar el elemento desconocido.

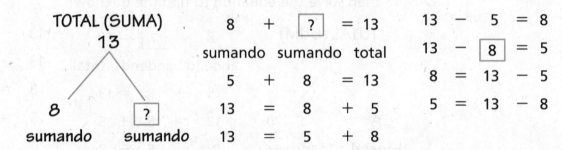

Se hace énfasis en las ecuaciones que tienen números solos en el lado izquierdo, para facilitar la comprensión del álgebra.

Para resolver problemas con una cantidad que es más o menos que otra, se usan **Barras de comparación**. Estas barras sirven para organizar la información del problema, y hallar así, la cantidad desconocida más pequeña, la más grande o la diferencia.

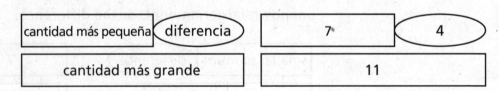

Si tiene alguna pregunta o algún comentario, por favor comuníquese conmigo.

Atentamente,
El maestro de su niño

© Houghton Mifflin Harcourt Publishing Company

 COMMON CORE Esta unidad incluye los Common Core Standards for Mathematical Content for Operations and Algebraic Thinking, CC.3.OA.3, CC.3.OA.4, CC.3.OA.8; Numbers and Operations in Base Ten, CC.3.NBT.1, CC.3.NBT.2, CC.3.NBT.3 and for all Mathematical Practices.

VOCABULARY
expression
equation
addend
sum
product

▶ Vocabulary

Choose the best word from the box.

1. An _____ is a mathematical sentence with an equal sign. (Lesson 5-1)

2. The _____ is the answer when adding two or more addends. (Lesson 5-1)

3. One of the numbers to be added is called a (an) _____. (Lesson 5-1)

▶ Concepts and Skills

Complete.

Show your work.

4. Elsa read 13 books this month.
She read 6 fewer books than Cliff read.
How many books did Cliff read?
Draw comparison bars to represent
the problem. (Lessons 5-4, 5-5)

_____

_____

5. Mr. Jackson set up some chairs in rows. He put the same number in each of 7 rows and put 7 chairs in the last row. He set up 70 chairs. How many did he put in each of the 7 rows? Explain how to write an equation and solve the problem. (Lessons 5-8, 5-9, 5-10, 5-11)

_____

_____

_____

_____

Complete.

6. Julie and Sam grew tomatoes. Julie grew
   160 plants. How many more tomatoes did Julie
   grow than Sam? What information do you need to
   solve the problem? Write the necessary information
   and solve the problem. (Lesson 5-6)

   _____

   _____

▶ Problem Solving

Write an equation and solve the problem.
(Lessons 5-6, 5-8, 5-9, 5-10, 5-11)

7. Becky has 20 fish and 2 hamsters.
   There are 8 angelfish and the
   rest are goldfish. She gets a
   number more goldfish. She
   now has 19 goldfish. How many
   goldfish did she get?

8. Raj is going on vacation for
   2 weeks and 5 days. How
   many days will he be on
   vacation?

   _____   _____

9. Paco made 33 belts and gave 5 away. He put the
   rest on 7 hangers with an equal number on each
   hanger. How many belts are on each hanger?

   _____

10. **Extended Response** Jason has 452 toy dinosaurs
    in his collection. His sister gave him 38 more toy
    dinosaurs. He sold a number of them. He now has
    418 toy dinosaurs. How many did he sell? Explain
    how you can decide if your answer is reasonable.

    _____

    _____

Dear Family,

Your student will be learning about geometry and measurement during this school year. This first part of Unit 6 is about the geometric figures called quadrilaterals. These get their name because they have four (*quad-*) sides (-*lateral*).

Here are some examples of quadrilaterals students will be learning about in this unit.

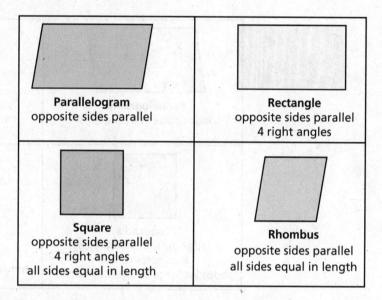

Parallelogram
opposite sides parallel

Rectangle
opposite sides parallel
4 right angles

Square
opposite sides parallel
4 right angles
all sides equal in length

Rhombus
opposite sides parallel
all sides equal in length

Students will be able to recognize and describe different quadrilaterals by their sides and angles. Some sides may be of equal length. Some sides may be parallel; they do not meet no matter how far they are extended. Some sides may be perpendicular; where they meet is like the corner of a square.

If you have any questions, please call or write to me.

Thank you.

Sincerely,
Your child's teacher

COMMON CORE This unit includes the Common Core Standards for Mathematical Content for Geometry, 3.G.1 and 3.G.2, and all Mathematical Practices.

Estimada familia:

Durante este año escolar, su niño aprenderá acerca de geometría y medición. La primera parte de la Unidad 6 trata sobre las figuras geométricas llamadas cuadriláteros. Se llaman así porque tienen cuatro (*quadri-*) lados (*-lateris*).

Aquí se muestran algunos ejemplos de cuadriláteros que los estudiantes estudiarán en esta unidad.

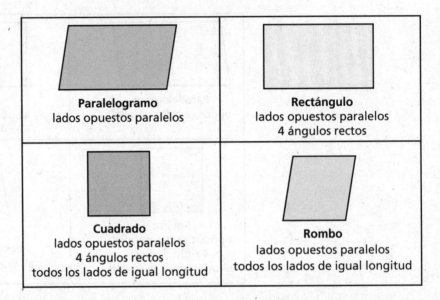

Paralelogramo
lados opuestos paralelos

Rectángulo
lados opuestos paralelos
4 ángulos rectos

Cuadrado
lados opuestos paralelos
4 ángulos rectos
todos los lados de igual longitud

Rombo
lados opuestos paralelos
todos los lados de igual longitud

Los estudiantes podrán reconocer y describir diferentes cuadriláteros según sus lados y ángulos. Algunos lados pueden tener la misma longitud. Algunos lados pueden ser paralelos; nunca se juntan, no importa cuánto se extiendan. Algunos lados pueden ser perpendiculares; donde se juntan es como el vértice de un cuadrado.

Si tiene alguna pregunta o algún comentario, por favor comuníquese conmigo.

Gracias.

Atentamente,
El maestro de su niño

COMMON CORE

Esta unidad incluye los Common Core Standards for Mathematical Content for Geometry, 3.G.1 and 3.G.2, and all Mathematical Practices.

VOCABULARY
quadrilateral

► Build Quadrilaterals from Triangles

A **quadrilateral** is a figure with 4 sides.

Cut out each pair of triangles. Use each pair to make as many different quadrilaterals as you can. You may flip a triangle and use the back. On a separate piece of paper, trace each quadrilateral that you make.

Triangles with One Angle Larger Than a Right Angle

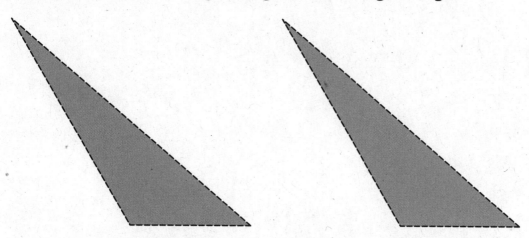

Triangles with Three Angles Smaller Than a Right Angle

Triangles with One Right Angle

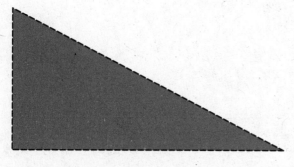
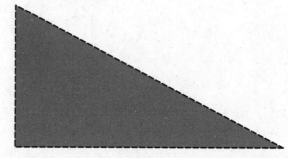

Triangles

▶ Build Polygons from Triangles

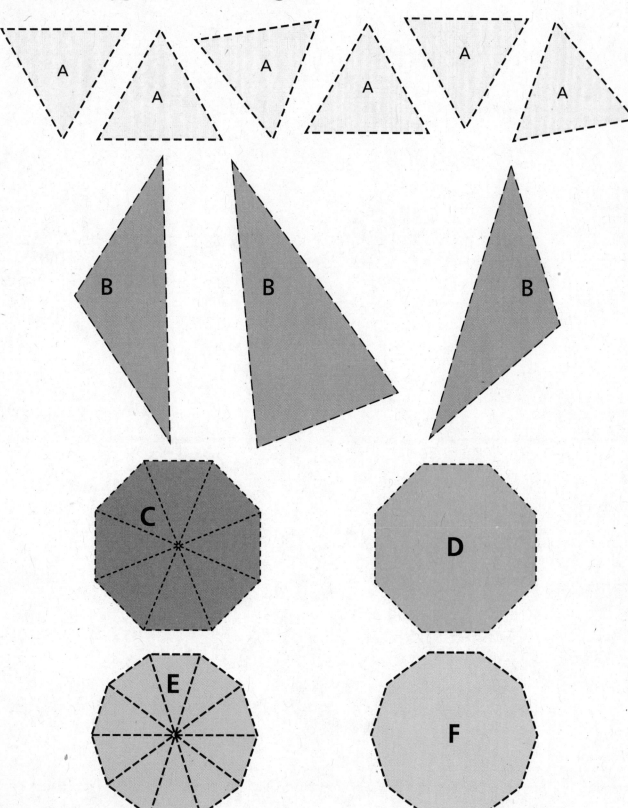

Triangles

▶ Draw Parallelograms

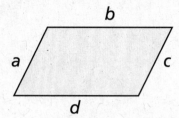

1. Write what you know about the opposite sides of a parallelogram.

_____

_____

2. Draw three different parallelograms.

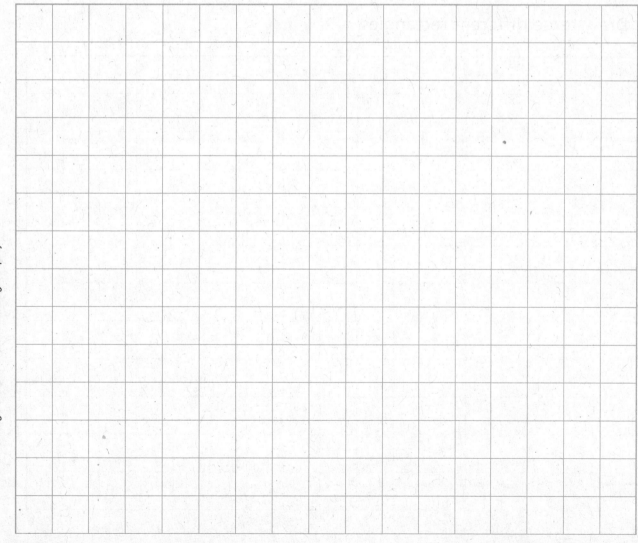

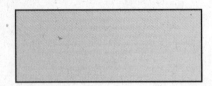

VOCABULARY
adjacent sides

▶ Draw Rectangles

3. Write everything you know about the opposite sides
   of a rectangle.

   _____

4. What do you know about the **adjacent sides**
   of a rectangle?

   _____

5. Draw three different rectangles.

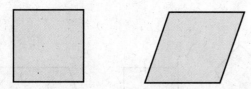

► Draw Squares and Rhombuses

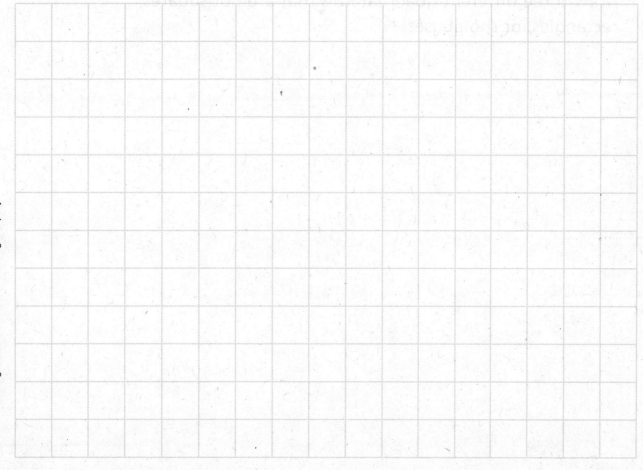

6. Write everything you know about squares.

_____

7. Write all you know about rhombuses.

_____

8. Draw two different squares and two
   different rhombuses.

► Draw Quadrilaterals That Are Not Squares, Rectangles, or Rhombuses

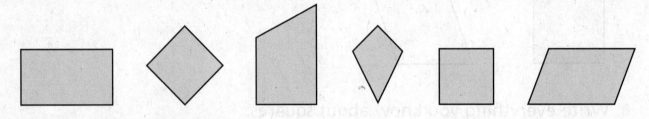

9. What is a quadrilateral?

_____

10. Name all the quadrilaterals that have at least one pair of parallel sides.

_____

11. Draw three different quadrilaterals that are not squares, rectangles, or rhombuses.

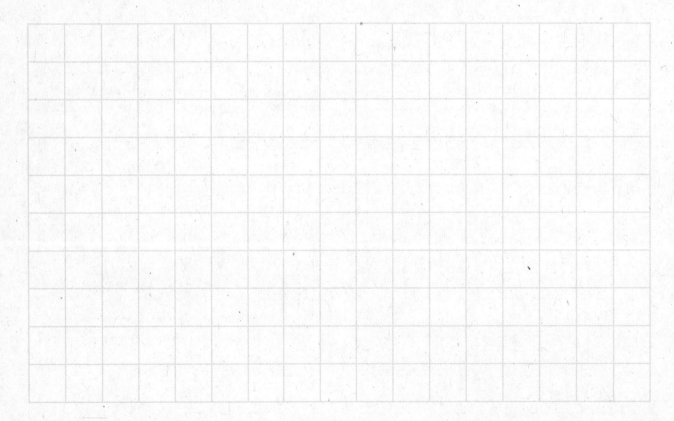

▶ Name Quadrilaterals

Place a check mark beside every name that describes the figure.

1.

- [ ] quadrilateral
- [ ] parallelogram
- [ ] rhombus
- [ ] rectangle
- [ ] square

2.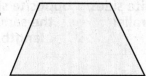

- [ ] quadrilateral
- [ ] parallelogram
- [ ] rhombus
- [ ] rectangle
- [ ] trapezoid

3.

- [ ] quadrilateral
- [ ] parallelogram
- [ ] rhombus
- [ ] rectangle
- [ ] square

4.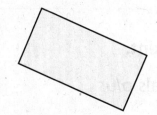

- [ ] quadrilateral
- [ ] parallelogram
- [ ] rhombus
- [ ] rectangle
- [ ] square

5.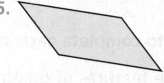

- [ ] quadrilateral
- [ ] parallelogram
- [ ] rhombus
- [ ] rectangle
- [ ] square

6.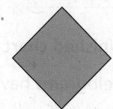

- [ ] quadrilateral
- [ ] parallelogram
- [ ] rhombus
- [ ] rectangle
- [ ] square

7.

- [ ] quadrilateral
- [ ] parallelogram
- [ ] rhombus
- [ ] rectangle
- [ ] square

8.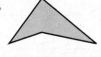

- [ ] quadrilateral
- [ ] parallelogram
- [ ] rhombus
- [ ] rectangle
- [ ] square

9.

- [ ] quadrilateral
- [ ] parallelogram
- [ ] rhombus
- [ ] rectangle
- [ ] square

▶ Analyze Quadrilaterals

10. For each figure, put Xs under the descriptions that are always true.

	Four sides	Both pairs of opposite sides parallel	Both pairs of opposite sides the same length	Four right angles	All sides the same length
Quadrilateral					
Trapezoid					
Parallelogram					
Rhombus					
Rectangle					
Square					

Use the finished chart above to complete each statement.

11. Parallelograms have all the features of quadrilaterals *plus*

_____

_____

12. Rectangles have all the features of parallelograms *plus*

_____

13. Squares have all the features of quadrilaterals *plus*

_____

_____

14. Trapezoids have all the features of quadrilaterals *plus*

_____

► **Draw Quadrilaterals from a Description**

Draw each figure.

15. Draw a quadrilateral that is *not* a parallelogram.

16. Draw a parallelogram that is *not* a rectangle.

17. Draw a rectangle that is *not* a square.

► **What's the Error?**

Dear Math Students,

Today I had to draw a quadrilateral with parallel sides that is not a rectangle, square, or rhombus. This is my drawing.

Is my drawing correct? If not, please help me understand why it is wrong.

Your friend,
Puzzled Penguin

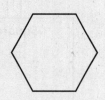

18. Write an answer to Puzzled Penguin.

_____

_____

▶ Sort and Classify Quadrilaterals

Use the category diagram to sort the figures you cut
out from Student Book page 315A. Write the letter
of the figure in the diagram to record your work.

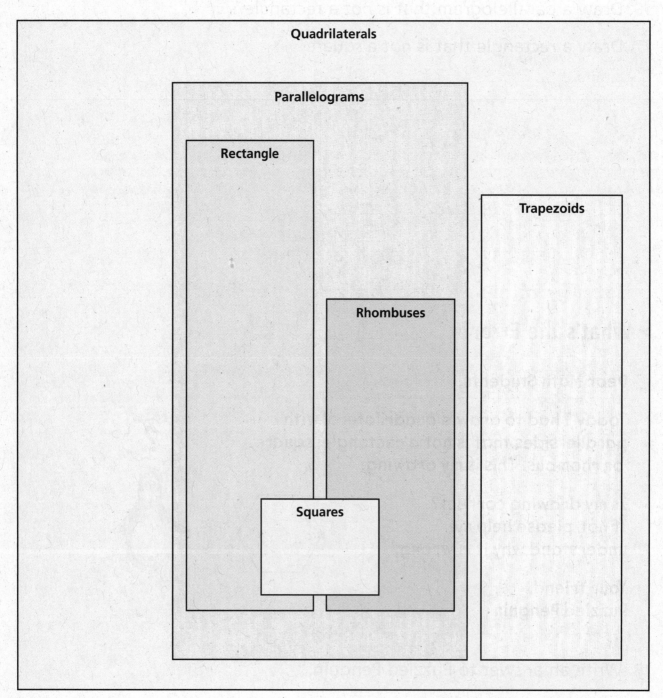

Name _____ **Date** _____

▶ Quadrilaterals for Sorting

Cut along the dashed lines.

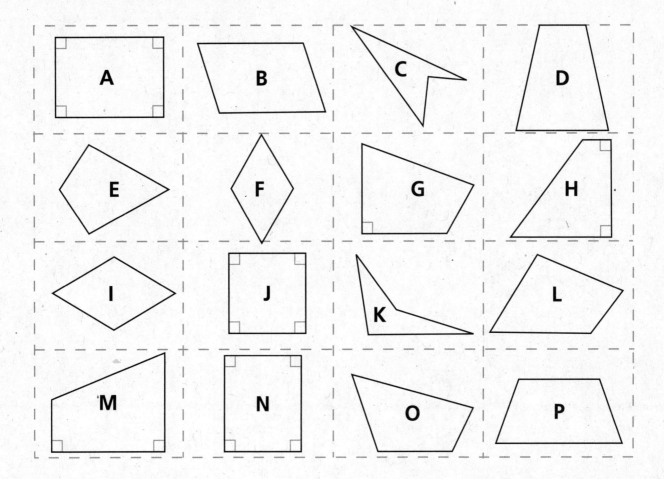

Classify Quadrilaterals **175**

Classify Quadrilaterals

Dear Family,

Your child is currently learning about perimeter and area. Students begin to investigate the area of a rectangle by counting the number of square units inside the figure. Students also find the perimeter of a rectangle by counting linear units around the outside of the figure.

Students develop methods to find the perimeter and area of a rectangle, as shown below.

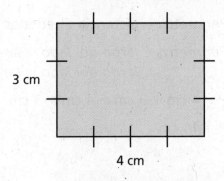

Perimeter = distance around the rectangle

Perimeter = side length + side length + side length + side length

P = 4 cm + 3 cm + 4 cm + 3 cm

P = 14 cm

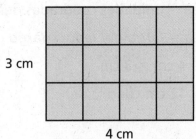

Area = square units inside the rectangle

Area = side length × side length

A = 4 cm × 3 cm

A = 12 sq cm

Students draw rectangles that have the same perimeter but different areas and rectangles that have the same area but different perimeters. They discover relationships between perimeter and area, such as that for a given area, the longest, skinniest rectangle has the greatest perimeter and the rectangle with sides closest to the same length or the same length has the least perimeter.

Students create shapes with tangrams, explore area relationships among the tangram shapes, and use the shapes as improvised units to measure area.

Throughout the unit students apply what they have learned about perimeter and area to real world problems.

If you have any questions or comments, please call or write to me.

Thank you.

Sincerely,
Your child's teacher

© Houghton Mifflin Harcourt Publishing Company

COMMON CORE This unit includes the Common Core Standards for Mathematical Content for Measurement and Data 3.MD.5, 3.MD.5a, 3.MD.5b, 3.MD.6, 3.MD.7, 3.MD.7a, 3.MD.7b, 3.MD.8, and all Mathematical Practices.

Estimada familia:

Su niño está aprendiendo acerca de perímetro y área. Los estudiantes comenzarán a investigar el área de un rectángulo contando las unidades cuadradas que caben en la figura. También hallarán el perímetro de un rectángulo contando las unidades lineales alrededor de la figura.

Los estudiantes desarrollarán métodos para hallar el perímetro y el área de un rectángulo, como se muestra a continuación.

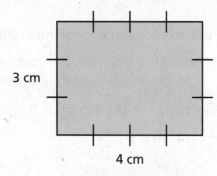

3 cm

4 cm

Perímetro = distancia alrededor del rectángulo

Perímetro = largo del lado + largo del lado + largo del lado + largo del lado

$P = 4 \text{ cm} + 3 \text{ cm} + 4 \text{ cm} + 3 \text{ cm}$

$P = 14 \text{ cm}$

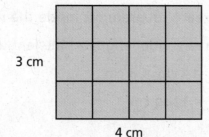

3 cm

4 cm

Área = unidades cuadradas dentro del rectángulo

Área = largo del lado × largo del lado

$A = 4 \text{ cm} \times 3 \text{ cm}$

$A = 12 \text{ cm cuad}$

Los estudiantes dibujarán rectángulos con el mismo perímetro pero diferentes áreas y rectángulos con la misma área pero diferentes perímetros. Descubrirán cómo se relacionan el perímetro y el área, por ejemplo, para un área determinada, el rectángulo más largo y angosto tiene el perímetro mayor y el rectángulo con lados de igual o casi igual longitud, tiene el perímetro menor.

Los estudiantes crearán figuras con tangramas, explorarán la relación entre el área de esas figuras y las usarán como medidas improvisadas para medir área.

Durante esta unidad los estudiantes aplicarán a problemas cotidianos lo que han aprendido acerca del perímetro y el área.

Si tiene alguna duda o algún comentario, por favor comuníquese conmigo.

Atentamente,
El maestro de su niño

© Houghton Mifflin Harcourt Publishing Company

▶ Recognize Perimeter and Area

**On this page, the dots on the dot paper are
1 cm apart. Use the rectangle for Exercises 1–4.**

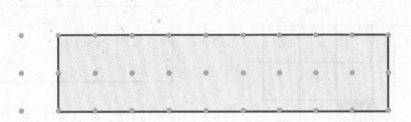

1. What part of the rectangle is its **perimeter**?

_____

2. What part of the rectangle is its **area**?

_____

3. Find the perimeter. Draw tick marks to help.

_____

4. Find the area. Draw **unit squares** to help.

_____

5. Draw a rectangle 5 cm long and 3 cm wide on the dot paper. Find the perimeter and area.

6. Explain how you found the area of the rectangle in Exercise 5.

_____

_____

_____

_____

Perimeter _____

Area _____

► Find Perimeter and Area

Find the perimeter and area of each figure.
Remember to include the correct units in your answers.

7.

perimeter   area

1 sq cm

⊢1 cm⊣

Perimeter = _____

Area = _____

8.

Perimeter = _____

Area = _____

9.

Perimeter = _____

Area = _____

10.

Perimeter = _____

Area = _____

11.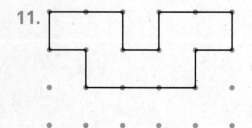

Perimeter = _____

Area = _____

12.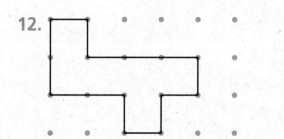

Perimeter = _____

Area = _____

Perimeter and Area

▶ Tile a Rectangle

**Cut out the 1-inch unit squares along the dashed lines.
Try to cut as carefully and as straight as you can.**

▶ Tile a Rectangle

13. Use the 1-inch unit squares from page
319A to cover the rectangle below.

14. Check whether there are any gaps
between the unit squares.

_____

15. Check whether any unit squares overlap.

_____

16. Draw lines to show the unit squares.
The number of unit squares is the area
in square inches. What is the area?

_____

17. Use an inch ruler to measure the side lengths
of the rectangle. Label the length and the width.

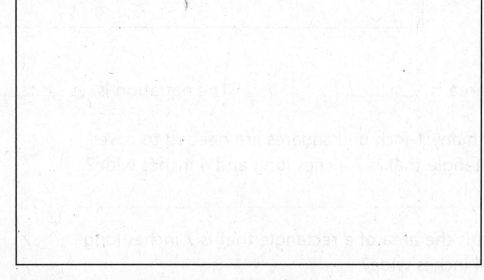

18. Write a multiplication equation to show the area.

_____

▶ Tile a Rectangle (continued)

**Cover each rectangle with 1-inch unit squares.
Count the squares to find the area. Then write
an equation to show the area.**

19.

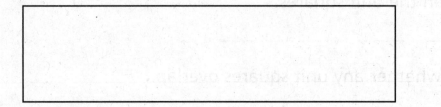

The area is _____   The equation is _____

20.

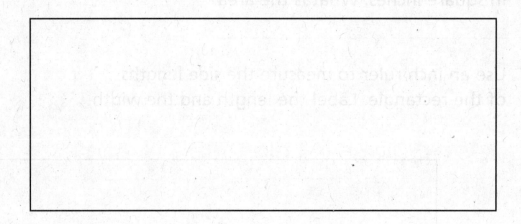

The area is _____   The equation is _____

21. How many 1-inch unit squares are needed to cover
a rectangle that is 7 inches long and 4 inches wide?

_____

22. What is the area of a rectangle that is 7 inches long
and 4 inches wide?

_____

Perimeter and Area

▶ Write Different Equations for Area

1. Use the drawings. Show two ways to find the area of a rectangle that is 10 units long and 6 units wide.

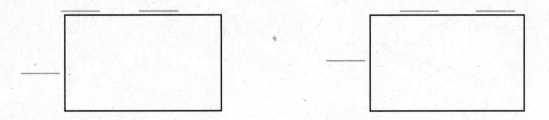

2. Write equations for your two rectangle drawings.

_____   _____

3. Suppose the rectangle is 10 feet long and 6 feet wide. What is its area?

_____

4. Suppose the rectangle is 10 meters long and 6 meters wide. What is its area?

_____

5. Use drawings and write equations to show two ways to find the area of a rectangle that is 9 yards long and 5 yards wide.

_____   _____

► Compare Rectangles with the Same Perimeter

Complete.

1. On a centimeter dot grid, draw all possible rectangles with a perimeter of 12 cm and sides whose lengths are whole centimeters. Label the lengths of two adjacent sides of each rectangle.

2. Find and label the area of each rectangle. In the table, record the lengths of the adjacent sides and the area of each rectangle.

3. Compare the shapes of the rectangles with the least and greatest areas.

Rectangles with Perimeter 12 cm	
Lengths of Two Adjacent Sides	Area

4. On a centimeter dot grid, draw all possible rectangles with a perimeter of 22 cm and sides whose lengths are whole centimeters. Label the lengths of two adjacent sides of each rectangle.

5. Find and label the area of each rectangle. In the table, record the lengths of the adjacent sides and the area of each rectangle.

6. Compare the shapes of the rectangles with the least and greatest areas.

Rectangles with Perimeter 22 cm	
Lengths of Two Adjacent Sides	Area

► **Compare Rectangles with the Same Area**

Complete.

7. On a centimeter dot grid, draw all possible
   rectangles with an area of 12 sq cm and sides
   whose lengths are whole centimeters. Label the
   lengths of two adjacent sides of each rectangle.

8. Find and label the perimeter of
   each rectangle. In the table,
   record the lengths of the adjacent
   sides and the perimeter of each
   rectangle.

9. Compare the shapes of the
   rectangles with the least
   and greatest perimeter.

| Rectangles with Area 12 sq cm ||
Lengths of Two Adjacent Sides	Perimeter

_____

_____

10. On a centimeter dot grid, draw all possible rectangles with
    an area of 18 sq cm and sides whose lengths are whole
    centimeters. Label the lengths of two adjacent sides of
    each rectangle.

11. Find and label the perimeter of
    each rectangle. In the table,
    record the lengths of the adjacent
    sides and the perimeter of each
    rectangle.

12. Compare the shapes of the
    rectangles with the least and greatest perimeter.

| Rectangles with Area 18 sq cm ||
Lengths of Two Adjacent Sides	Perimeter

_____

_____

▶ Find Area by Decomposing into Rectangles

Decompose each figure into rectangles.
Then find the area of the figure.

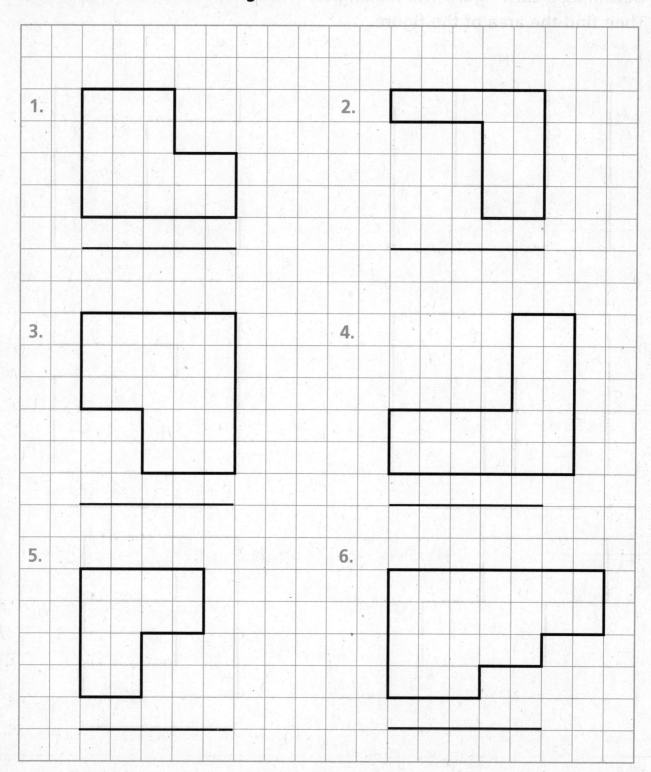

1.

2.

3.

4.

5.

6.

► Find Area by Decomposing into Rectangles (continued)

Decompose each figure into rectangles.
Then find the area of the figure.

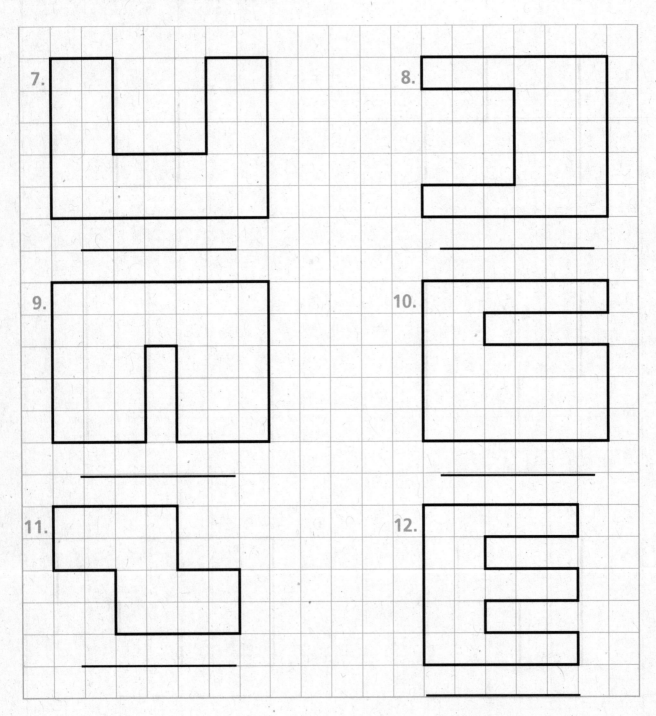

7.

8.

9.

10.

11.

12.

▶ Find Area by Decomposing into Rectangles (continued)

Decompose each figure into rectangles.
Then find the area of the figure.

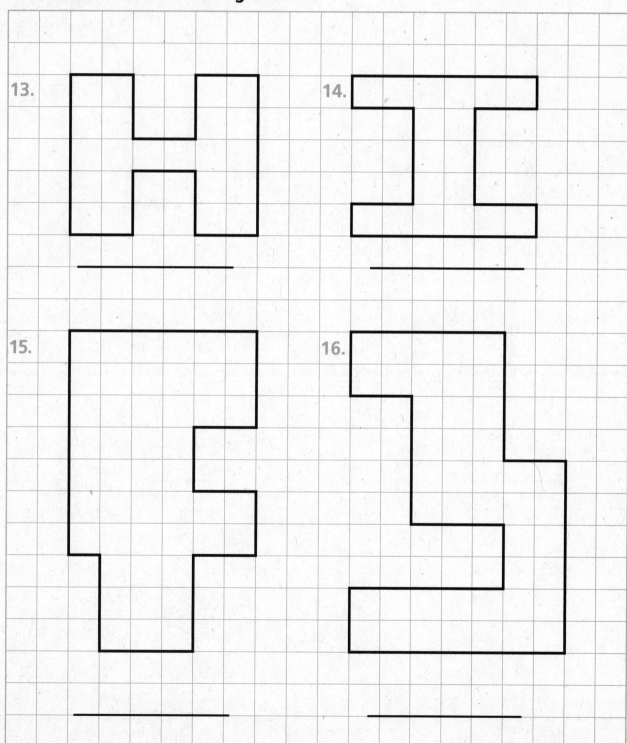

13. _____

14. _____

15. _____

16. _____

▶ Explore Tangrams

Cut one tangram figure into pieces along the dotted lines.
Try to cut as carefully and as straight as you can. Save the
other figures to use later.

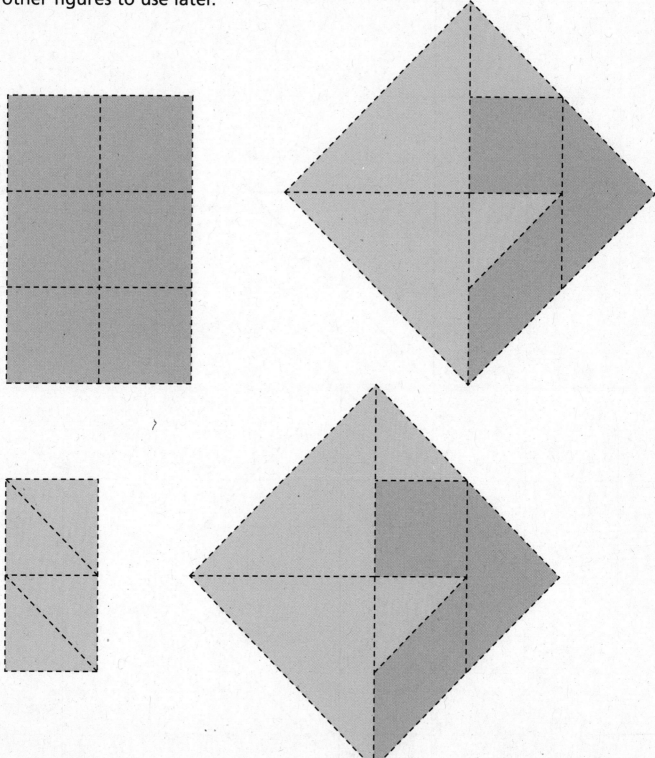

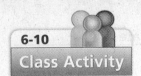
▶ Explore Tangrams (continued)

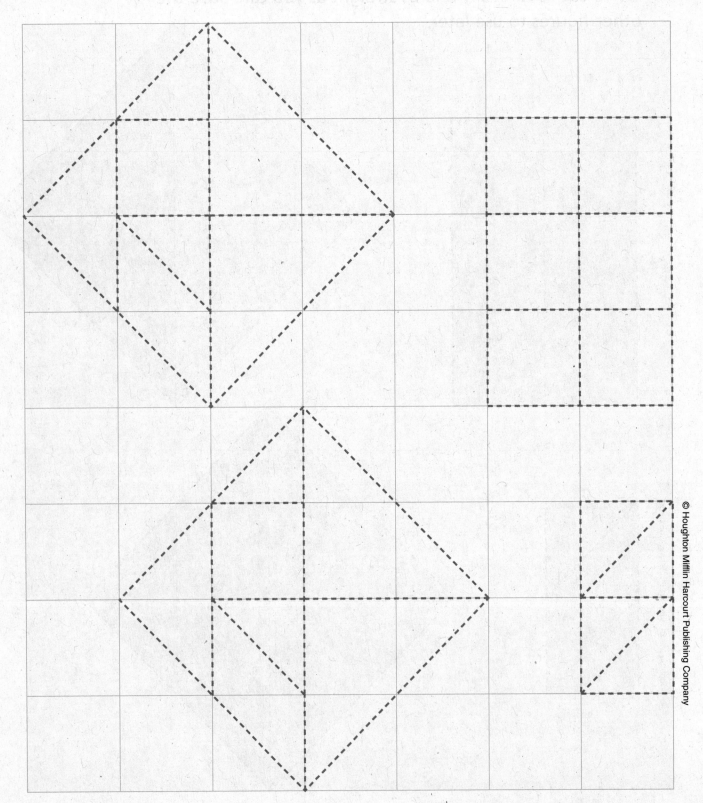

Tangram Shapes and Area

▶ Solve Tangram Puzzles

Use the tangram pieces from page 335A.

1. Make this bird. When you finish, draw lines to show how you placed the pieces.

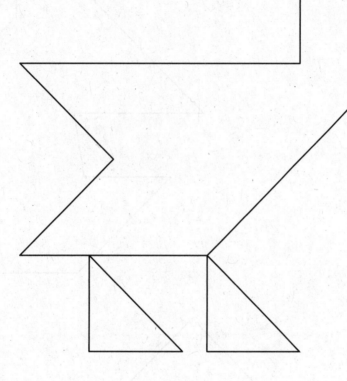

2. Make this rectangle. Draw lines to show how you placed the pieces. Hint: You do not need all the pieces.

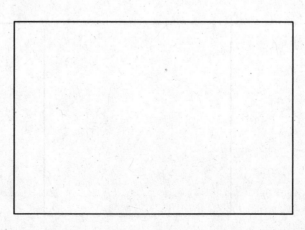

▶ Solve Tangram Puzzles (continued)

Use the tangram pieces. Draw lines to show how you placed the pieces.

3. Make this boat.

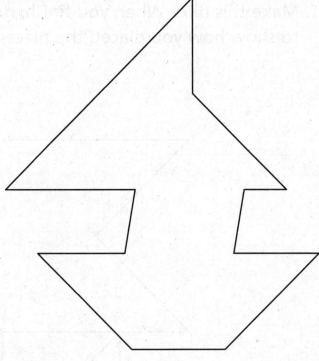

4. Make this tree.

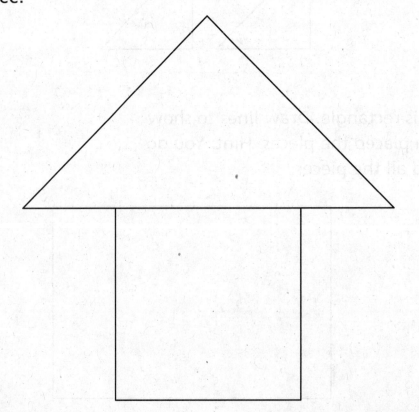

▶ Use Tangram Pieces to Find Area

5. Use the seven tangram pieces. Cover this rectangle.

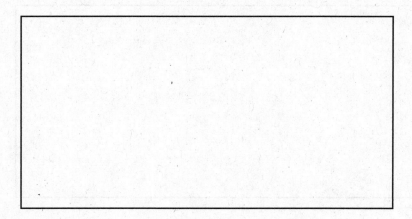

6. What is the area of the rectangle?

_____

7. Use any tangram pieces. Cover this rectangle.

8. What is the area of the rectangle?

_____

▶ Use Tangram Pieces to Find Area (continued)

Use any tangram pieces. Cover each rectangle.

9.

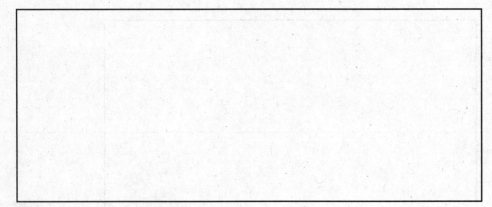

What is the area of the rectangle?

_____

10.

What is the area of the square?

_____

Tangram Shapes and Area

▶ **Use Tangram Pieces to Find Area (continued)**

Use any tangram pieces. Cover each figure.

11.

12.

What is the area of the square?

_____

What is the area of the rectangle?

_____

13.

What is the area of the figure?

_____

► **Use Tangram Pieces to Find Area (continued)**

Use any tangram pieces. Cover each figure.

14.

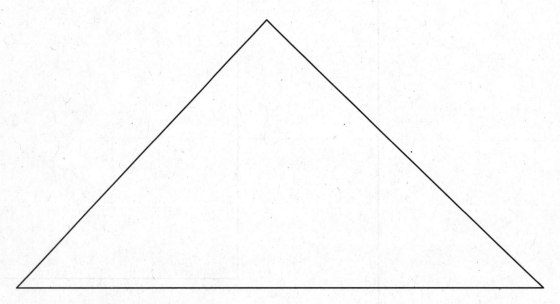

What is the area of the triangle?

_____

15.

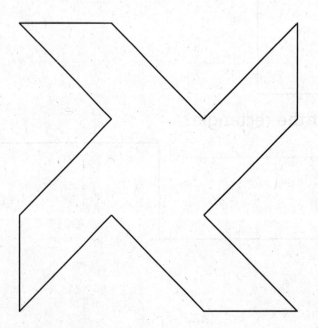

What is the area of the figure?

_____

▶ Math and Gardening

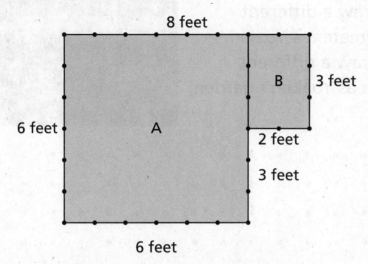

Look at the drawing of Yoakim's garden.
It is divided into two quadrilaterals.

1. What is the perimeter of part A? _____

   What is the perimeter of part B? _____

2. What is the perimeter of the combined
   garden? _____

3. Will Yoakim need more fencing to enclose the two
   parts of his garden separately or to enclose the
   combined garden?

   _____

4. What is the area of part A? _____

   What is the area of part B? _____

5. What is the area of the combined garden?

   _____

6. How does the total area of the two parts of the garden
   compare to the area of the combined garden?

   _____

▶ Design a Garden

Use the dot paper below to draw a different garden that has the same perimeter as Yoakim's combined garden. Beside it, draw a different garden that has the same area as Yoakim's garden.

⊢1 ft⊣

7. What is the area of your garden that has the same perimeter as Yoakim's garden?

_____

8. What is the perimeter of your garden that has the same area as Yoakim's garden?

_____

9. Use the centimeter dot paper at the right to draw separate areas within a garden where you would plant corn, beans, and tomatoes.

The area for corn is 12 square feet.
The area for beans is 25 square feet.
The area for tomatoes is 20 square feet.

▶ Vocabulary

Choose the best word from the box.

1. A _____ is a four-sided figure with 4 right angles. (Lesson 6-2)

2. The _____ of a figure is the number of square units in the figure. (Lesson 6-5)

3. A _____ is a parallelogram with all sides equal. (Lesson 6-2)

4. The _____ of a figure is the distance around it. (Lesson 6-5)

▶ Concepts and Skills

5. To which larger category do parallelograms, rectangles, squares, rhombuses, and trapezoids belong? Explain. (Lesson 6-4)

_____

_____

6. How is area measured? (Lesson 6-5)

_____

_____

7. Show all the ways you can use to find the area of the rectangle at the right. (Lessons 6-5, 6-6, 6-10)

_____

_____

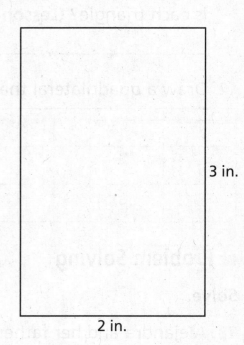

3 in.

2 in.

Put a check mark beside every name that describes the figure. (Lessons 6-2, 6-3, 6-4)

8.

☐ quadrilateral

☐ not a quadrilateral

☐ rectangle

☐ square

9.

☐ quadrilateral

☐ not a quadrilateral

☐ rectangle

☐ square

10.

☐ quadrilateral

☐ not a quadrilateral

☐ rectangle

☐ square

11. This hexagon has been divided into triangles with equal areas. What part of the area of the hexagon is each triangle? (Lesson 6-10)

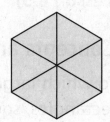

_____

12. Draw a quadrilateral that is not a rectangle, square, or rhombus.

▶ Problem Solving

Solve.

13. Alejandra and her father tiled a bathroom floor. They used 48 tiles that measure 1 foot on a side. One side of the bathroom is 8 ft. How long is the other side? (Lesson 6-6)

_____

14. Victor and his mother are making a rectangular corral for a pony. They used 66 feet of fencing. One side has 15 feet of fencing. How many feet of fencing does the other side have? (Lesson 6-6)

_____

15. Dory is designing a sticker. She wants the sticker to have a perimeter of 14 cm. On the dot grid, draw all possible rectangles whose side lengths are whole centimeters. Label the lengths of the two adjacent sides of each rectangle. Label each rectangle with its area. (Lesson 6-7)

16. Jacob is designing a package label. He wants the area to be 12 square cm. On the dot grid, draw all possible rectangles whose side lengths are whole centimeters. Label the lengths of the two adjacent sides of each rectangle. Label each rectangle with its perimeter. (Lesson 6-7)

Solve.

17. Deshawn wants to build a fence around a rectangular garden. The garden is 5 yards long and 3 yards wide. The fence sections are 1 yard long. How many sections of fence does Deshawn need? What is the area of the garden? (Lessons 6-5, 6-9)

Perimeter: _____

Area: _____

18. Liana wants to put a rope around two rectangular spaces next to each other in her yard for a garden. One space is 5 meters long and 6 meters wide. The other space is 3 meters long and 6 meters wide. How much rope does Liana need? What will be the area of the garden? (Lessons 6-5, 6-6, 6-9, 6-10)

Perimeter: _____

Area: _____

19. A sandbox is in the shape of a pentagon. Each side is 5 feet long. How much wood is needed to go around the sandbox? (Lessons 6-2, 6-9)

_____

20. Extended Response David and his mother are sewing a quilt together from squares 1 foot on a side. David's mother will sew a 3 feet by 5 feet section of the quilt. David will sew a 4 feet by 5 feet section of the quilt. What will the area of the quilt be? Explain how you found the answer. Draw a picture of the quilt to show your answer is correct. (Lessons 6-8, 6-11)

_____

_____

_____

Family Letter

Dear Family,

In this unit, your child will be introduced to fractions. Students will build fractions from unit fractions and explore fractions as parts of a whole.

Unit Fraction

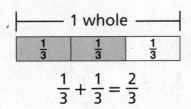

$$\frac{1}{3} + \frac{1}{3} = \frac{2}{3}$$

Fraction of a Whole

$\frac{3}{4}$ ← numerator
— denominator

Students will find equivalent fractions, and compare fractions with either the same denominator or the same numerator.

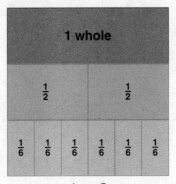

$$\frac{1}{2} = \frac{3}{6}$$

$$\frac{1}{2} > \frac{1}{6}$$

$$\frac{2}{4} < \frac{3}{4}$$

In this unit, your child will also solve real world problems using his or her understanding of fraction concepts.

Please call if you have any questions or comments.

Sincerely,
Your child's teacher

COMMON CORE

This unit includes the Common Core Standards for Mathematical Content for Numbers and Operations–Fractions, CC.3.NF.1, CC.3.NF.2a, CC.3.NF.2b, CC.3.NF.3a, CC.3.NF.3b, CC.3.NF.3c, CC.3.NF.3d; Geometry, CC.3.G.2 and for all Mathematical Practices.

Estimada familia:

En esta unidad, se le presentarán por primera vez las fracciones a su niño. Los estudiantes formarán fracciones con fracciones unitarias y explorarán las fracciones como partes de un entero.

Fracción unitaria

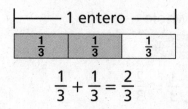

$$\frac{1}{3} + \frac{1}{3} = \frac{2}{3}$$

Fracción de un entero

$$\frac{3}{4} \begin{array}{l} \leftarrow \text{numerador} \\ \leftarrow \text{denominador} \end{array}$$

Los estudiantes hallarán fracciones equivalentes y compararán fracciones del mismo denominador o del mismo numerador.

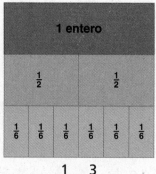

$$\frac{1}{2} = \frac{3}{6}$$

$$\frac{1}{2} > \frac{1}{6}$$

$$\frac{2}{4} < \frac{3}{4}$$

En esta unidad, su niño también resolverá problemas cotidianos usando los conceptos que aprenda sobre fracciones.

Si tiene alguna duda o algún comentario, por favor comuníquese conmigo.

Atentamente,
El maestro de su niño

COMMON CORE

Esta unidad incluye los Common Core Standards for Mathematical Content for Numbers and Operations–Fractions, CC.3.NF.1, CC.3.NF.2a, CC.3.NF.2b, CC.3.NF.3a, CC.3.NF.3b, CC.3.NF.3c, CC.3.NF.3d; Geometry, CC.3.G.2 and for all Mathematical Practices.

▶ Fraction Rectangles

Cut out the bottom rectangle first.
Then cut on the dotted lines to make 4 rectangles.
Wait to cut out the top rectangle.

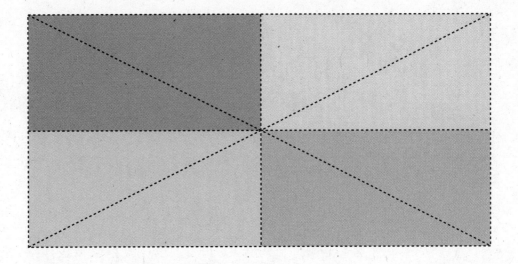

Understand Fractions

▶ Unit Fractions and Fraction Bars

You can represent a **fraction** with a fraction bar. The **denominator** tells how many equal parts the whole is divided into. The **numerator** tells how many equal parts you are talking about.

1 whole

$\dfrac{1}{3}$ ← numerator
← denominator

Shade 1 part.

A **unit fraction** has a numerator of 1. Shade the rest of the fraction bars at the right below to represent unit fractions. What patterns do you see?

| 1 whole | → | | 1   one |

Divide the whole into 2 equal parts. → Shade 1 part. $\dfrac{1}{2}$ one half

Divide the whole into 3 equal parts. → Shade 1 part. $\dfrac{1}{3}$ one third

Divide the whole into 4 equal parts. → Shade 1 part. $\dfrac{1}{4}$ one fourth

Divide the whole into 5 equal parts. → Shade 1 part. $\dfrac{1}{5}$ one fifth

Divide the whole into 6 equal parts. → Shade 1 part. $\dfrac{1}{6}$ one sixth

Divide the whole into 7 equal parts. → Shade 1 part. $\dfrac{1}{7}$ one seventh

Divide the whole into 8 equal parts. → Shade 1 part. $\dfrac{1}{8}$ one eighth

► Build Fractions from Unit Fractions

Write the unit fractions for each whole. Next, shade the correct number of parts. Then show each shaded fraction as a sum of unit fractions.

9. [| | | | |] → Shade 2 parts.
   Divide the whole into 5 equal parts.

   $$\frac{1}{5} + \frac{1}{5} + \frac{1}{5} + \frac{1}{5} + \frac{1}{5}$$ $$\frac{1}{5} + \frac{1}{5} = \frac{2}{5}$$

10. [| |] → [| |] Shade 2 parts.
    Divide the whole into 3 equal parts.

    _____

11. [| | | | | |] → [| | | | | |] Shade 5 parts.
    Divide the whole into 7 equal parts.

    _____

12. [| | | | | | |] → [| | | | | | |] Shade 7 parts.
    Divide the whole into 8 equal parts.

    _____

13. [| | | | |] → [| | | | |] Shade 3 parts.
    Divide the whole into 6 equal parts.

    _____

14. [| | | | | | |] → [| | | | | | |] Shade 8 parts.
    Divide the whole into 8 equal parts.

    _____

Understand Fractions

Name _____ Date _____

► Use Fraction Bars

Shade each fraction bar to show the fraction.
First, divide the fraction bar into the correct unit fractions.

1. $\frac{1}{6}$
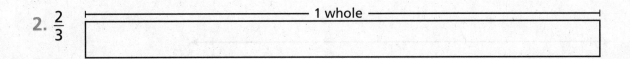
1 whole

2. $\frac{2}{3}$
1 whole

3. $\frac{7}{8}$
1 whole

4. $\frac{2}{4}$
1 whole

5. $\frac{5}{6}$
1 whole

6. $\frac{3}{8}$
1 whole

Model Fractions **213**

Name _____ Date _____

► Use Number Lines

Mark each number line to show the fraction.
First, divide the number line into the correct unit fractions.

7. $\frac{1}{6}$

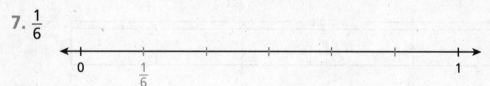

0     $\frac{1}{6}$ 1

8. $\frac{2}{3}$

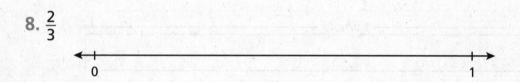

0   1

9. $\frac{7}{8}$

0   1

10. $\frac{2}{4}$

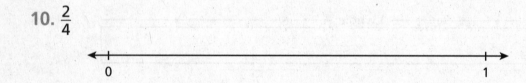

0   1

11. $\frac{5}{6}$

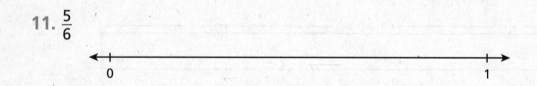

0   1

12. $\frac{3}{8}$

0   1

► **Locate Fractions Less Than 1**

Locate each fraction on the number line.
Draw more number lines if you need to.

1. $\frac{1}{4}$ |←———————————————————|→
       0   1

2. $\frac{1}{8}$ |←———————————————————|→
       0   1

3. $\frac{2}{3}$ |←———————————————————|→
       0   1

4. $\frac{5}{6}$ |←———————————————————|→
       0   1

5. $\frac{1}{6}$ and $\frac{2}{3}$ |←———————————————————|→
              0   1

6. $\frac{1}{3}$ and $\frac{5}{8}$ |←———————————————————|→
              0   1

7. $\frac{1}{6}$ and $\frac{3}{4}$ |←———————————————————|→
              0   1

▶ Locate Fractions Greater Than 1

Locate each fraction on the number line.

8. $\frac{5}{4}$

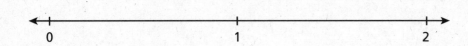

9. $\frac{8}{3}$

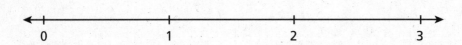

10. $\frac{5}{1}$

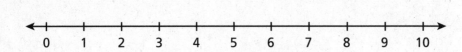

11. $\frac{8}{6}$

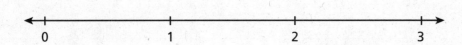

12. $\frac{6}{2}$

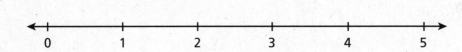

13. Explain how you located the fraction for one of the Exercises from 8–12.

_____

_____

_____

► Find 1

Locate 1 on each number line.

14.
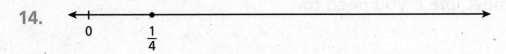

0   $\frac{1}{4}$

15.
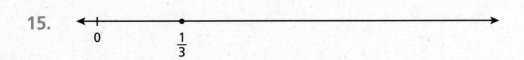

0   $\frac{1}{3}$

16.
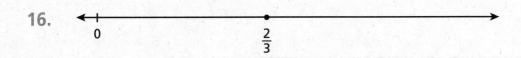

0   $\frac{2}{3}$

17.
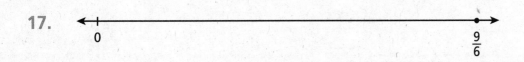

0   $\frac{9}{6}$

18.
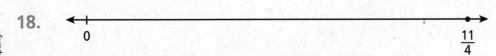

0   $\frac{11}{4}$

19. Explain how you located 1 for Exercise 17.

_____

_____

_____

▶ Find Fractions

Locate each fraction on the number line.
Draw another number line if you need to.

20. $\frac{3}{4}$

0                     $\frac{1}{2}$

21. $\frac{5}{6}$

0                     $\frac{10}{6}$

22. $\frac{2}{3}$

0           $\frac{1}{4}$

23. $\frac{7}{4}$

0                   $\frac{7}{6}$

24. $\frac{7}{8}$

0                          $\frac{2}{3}$

25. $\frac{10}{8}$

0                          $\frac{4}{2}$

► Fraction Circles

Label each unit fraction.
Then cut out the fraction
circles on the dashed lines.

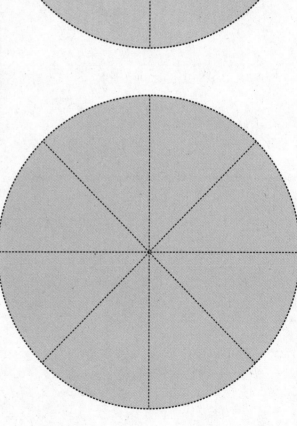

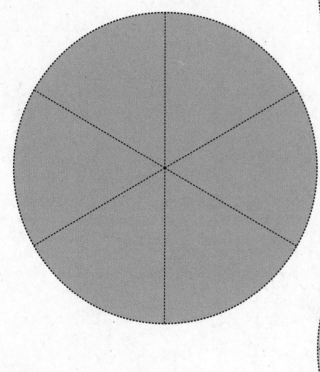

Name

Date

▶ Make Fraction Strips

Make Fraction Strips

Fraction Strips

VOCABULARY
equivalence chain

► Equivalent Fractions on Number Lines

1. Complete each number line. Show all fractions including each fraction for 1.

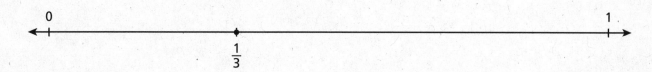

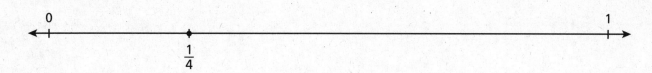

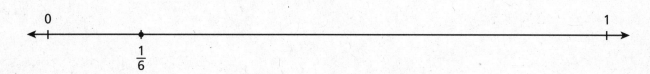

2. Write an equivalence chain with fractions that equal $\frac{2}{2}$.

_____

3. Why are the fractions in the equivalence chain for $\frac{2}{2}$ equal?

_____

4. Why does the length of unit fractions grow smaller as their denominators get larger?

_____

VOCABULARY
denominator
fraction
numerator
unit fraction

► Vocabulary

Choose the best word from the box.

1. A _____ is a number that names one part of a whole and has a numerator of 1. (Lesson 7-1)

2. The bottom number in a fraction that tells how many equal parts the whole is divided into is called the _____. (Lesson 7-1)

3. The top number in a fraction that tells how many of the equal parts you are talking about is called the _____. (Lesson 7-1)

► Concepts and Skills

4. What are two ways you can tell if two fractions are equivalent? (Lessons 7-6, 7-7)

   _____

   _____

5. Why is $\frac{1}{2}$ of a pizza larger than $\frac{1}{4}$ of the same size pizza? (Lesson 7-4)

   _____

   _____

6. Write the unit fraction for the whole. Next, shade the correct number of parts. Then, show the shaded fraction as a sum of unit fractions. (Lessons 7-1, 7-2)

   Divide the whole into 4 equal parts.

   _____

Mark the number line to show the fractions. First divide the number into correct unit fractions. (Lessons 7-2, 7-3, 7-8)

7. $\frac{1}{8}$ 8. $\frac{5}{8}$ 9. $\frac{8}{8}$ 10. $\frac{3}{4}$

Write an equivalence chain. Use your fraction strips or a number line if you need to. (Lessons 7-6, 7-7, 7-8)

11. With fractions that equal $\frac{1}{2}$ _____

12. With fractions that equal $\frac{6}{6}$ _____

Locate each fraction on the number line. (Lesson 7-3)

13. $\frac{3}{1}$ 14. $\frac{9}{6}$ 15. $\frac{4}{2}$

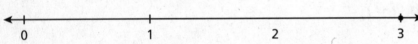

Compare. Use <, >, or =. (Lessons 7-4, 7-5)

16. $\frac{3}{8} \bigcirc \frac{5}{8}$ 17. $\frac{6}{3} \bigcirc \frac{6}{4}$ 18. $\frac{3}{3} \bigcirc \frac{2}{2}$

▶ **Problem Solving**

Solve. (Lessons 7-4, 7-5, 7-6, 7-7)

19. Diane's water bottle holds $\frac{5}{4}$ liter of water. Joe's holds $\frac{3}{4}$ liter of water. Whose water bottle holds more water? How do you know?

_____

20. **Extended Response** Dan walks $\frac{5}{8}$ mile to school. Beth walks $\frac{3}{4}$ mile to school. Who walks farther? Explain your answer. Show you are correct using the circles.

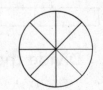

_____